The MAST MINᴅ

Napoleon Hill (1883-1970), best known for his global bestseller *Think and Grow Rich*, was a self-help author and businessman whose work has influenced millions across the world, from Norman Vincent Peale to Donald Trump. Born poor, Hill lived a colourful life, pursuing several different business ventures and professions. He also met and advised many famous people, such as US President Woodrow Wilson. Hill eventually found widespread success as a motivational author, writing several books on how to achieve success and practically creating the self-help genre.

The
MASTER
MIND

NAPOLEON HILL

RUPA

Published by
Rupa Publications India Pvt. Ltd 2024
7/16, Ansari Road, Daryaganj
New Delhi 110002

Sales centres:
Bengaluru Chennai
Hyderabad Jaipur Kathmandu
Kolkata Mumbai Prayagraj

P-ISBN: 978-93-6156-482-6

First impression 2024

10 9 8 7 6 5 4 3 2 1

Printed in India

CONTENTS

1

MASTERMIND

Success is very largely a matter of adjusting one's self to the ever-varying and changing environments of life, in a spirit of harmony and poise. Harmony is based upon understanding of the forces constituting one's environment; therefore, this course is in reality a blueprint that may be followed straight to success, because it helps the student to interpret, understand and make the most of these environmental forces of life.

The most successful men and women on earth have had to correct certain weak spots in their personalities before they began to succeed. The most outstanding of these weaknesses which stand between men and women and success are INTOLERANCE, CUPIDITY, GREED, JEALOUSY, SUSPICION, REVENGE, EGOTISM, CONCEIT, THE TENDENCY TO REAP WHERE THEY HAVE NOT SOWN, and the HABIT OF SPENDING MORE THAN THEY EARN.

All of these common enemies of mankind, and many more not here mentioned, are covered by the Law of Success course in such a manner that any person of reasonable intelligence may master them with but little effort or inconvenience.

You should know, at the very outset, that the Law of Success course has long since passed through the experimental state; that it already has to its credit a record of achievement that is worthy of serious thought and analysis. You should know, also, that the

Law of Success course has been examined and endorsed by some of the most practical minds of this generation.

The Law of Success course was first used as a lecture, and was delivered by its author in practically every city and in many of the smaller localities, throughout the United States, over a period of more than seven years. Perhaps you were one of the many hundreds of thousands of people who heard this lecture.

During these lectures the author had assistants located in the audiences for the purpose of interpreting the reaction of those who heard the lecture, and in this manner he learned exactly what effect it had upon people. As a result of this study and analysis many changes were made.

The first big victory was gained for the Law of Success philosophy when it was used by the author as the basis of a course with which 3,000 men and women were trained as a sales army. The majority of these people were without previous experience, of any sort, in the field of selling. Through this training they were enabled to earn more than One Million Dollars ($1,000,000.00) for themselves and paid the author $30,000.00 for his services, covering a period of approximately six months.

The individuals and small groups of salespeople who have found success through the aid of this course are too numerous to be mentioned in this Introduction, but the number is large and the benefits they derived from the course were definite.

The Law of Success philosophy was brought to the attention of the late Don R. Mellett, former publisher of the Canton (Ohio) Daily News, who formed a partnership with the author of the course and was preparing to resign as publisher of the Canton Daily News and take up the business management of the author's affairs when he was assassinated on July 16, 1926.

Prior to his death Mr. Mellett had made arrangements with judge Elbert H. Gary, who was then Chairman of the Board of the United States Steel Corporation, to present the Law of Success course to every employee of the Steel Corporation, at a total cost of something like $150,000.00. This plan was halted because of judge Gary's death, but it proves that the author of the Law of Success has produced an educational plan of an enduring nature. Judge Gary was eminently prepared to judge the value of such a course, and the fact that he analyzed the Law of Success philosophy and was preparing to invest the huge sum of $150,000.00 in it is proof of the soundness of all that is said in behalf of the course.

You will observe, in this General Introduction to the course, a few technical terms which may not be plain to you. Do not allow this to bother you. Make no attempt at first reading to understand these terms. They will be plain to you after you read the remainder of the course. This entire Introduction is intended only as a background for the other lessons of the course, and you should read it as such. You will not be examined on this Introduction, but you should read it many times, as you will get from it at each reading a thought or an idea which you did not get on previous readings.

In this Introduction you will find a description of a newly discovered law of psychology which is the very foundation stone of all outstanding personal achievements. This law has been referred to by the author as the "Master Mind," meaning a mind that is developed through the harmonious co-operation of two or more people who ally themselves for the purpose of accomplishing any given task.

If you are engaged in the business of selling you may profitably experiment with this law of the "Master Mind" in your daily work. It has been found that a group of six or seven salespeople may use the law so effectively that their sales may be increased to unbelievable proportions.

Life Insurance is supposed to be the hardest thing on earth to sell. This ought not to be true, with an established necessity such as life insurance, but it is. Despite this fact, a small group of men working for the Prudential Life Insurance Company, whose sales are mostly small policies, formed a little friendly group for the purpose of experimenting with the law of the "Master Mind," with the result that every man in the group wrote more insurance during the first three months of the experiment than he had ever written in an entire year before.

What may be accomplished through the aid of this principle, by any small group of intelligent life insurance salesmen who have learned how to apply the law of the "Master Mind" will stagger the imagination of the most highly optimistic and imaginative person.

The same may be said of other groups of salespeople who are engaged in selling merchandise and other more tangible forms of service than life insurance. Bear this in mind as you read this Introduction to the Law of Success course and it is not unreasonable to expect that this Introduction, alone, may give you sufficient understanding of the law to change the entire course of your life.

THE ART OF SELLING YOURSELF

It is the personalities back of a business which determine the measure of success the business will enjoy. Modify those personalities so they are more pleasing and more attractive to the patrons of the business and the business will thrive. In any of the great cities of the United States one may purchase merchandise of similar nature and price in scores of stores, yet you will find there is always one outstanding store which does more business than any of the others, and the reason for this is that back of that store is a man, or men, who has attended to the personalities of those who come in contact with the public. People buy personalities as much as merchandise, and it is a question if they are not influenced more by the personalities with which they come in contact than they are by the merchandise.

Life insurance has been reduced to such a scientific basis that the cost of insurance does not vary to any great extent, regardless of the company from which one purchases it, yet out of the hundreds of life insurance companies doing business less than a dozen companies do the bulk of the business of the United States.

Why? Personalities! Ninety-nine people out of every hundred who purchase life insurance policies do not know what is in their policies and, what seems more startling, do not seem to care. What they really purchase is the pleasing personality of some man or woman who knows the value of cultivating such a personality.

Your business in life, or at least the most important part of it, is to achieve success. Success, within the meaning of that term as covered by this course on the Fifteen Laws of Success, is "the attainment of your Definite Chief Aim without violating the rights of other people." Regardless of what your major aim in life may be, you will attain it with much less difficulty after you learn how to cultivate a pleasing personality and after you have learned the delicate art of allying yourself with others in a given undertaking without friction or envy.

One of the greatest problems of life, if not, in fact, the greatest, is that of learning the art of harmonious negotiation with others. This course was created for the purpose of teaching people how to negotiate their way through life with harmony and poise, free from the destructive effects of disagreement and friction which bring millions of people to misery, want and failure every year.

With this statement of the purpose of the course you should be able to approach the lessons with the feeling that a complete transformation is about to take place in your personality.

You cannot enjoy outstanding success in life without power, and you can never enjoy power without sufficient personality to influence other people to cooperate with you in a spirit of harmony.

The state of advancement known as "civilization" is but the measure of knowledge which the race has accumulated. This knowledge is of two classes—mental and physical.

Among the useful knowledge organized by man, he has discovered and catalogued the eighty-odd physical elements of which all material forms in the universe consist.

MIND'S BUILDING BLOCKS

By study and analysis and accurate measurements man has discovered the "bigness" of the material side of the universe as represented by planets, suns and stars, some of which are known to be over ten million times as large as the little earth on which he lives.

On the other hand, man has discovered the "littleness" of the physical forms which constitute the universe by reducing the eighty-odd physical elements to molecules, atoms, and, finally, to the smallest particle, the electron. An electron cannot be seen; it is but a center of force consisting of a positive or a negative. The electron is the beginning of everything of a physical nature.

MOLECULES, ATOMS AND ELECTRONS: To understand both the detail and the perspective of the process through which knowledge is gathered, organized and classified, it seems essential for the student to begin with the smallest and simplest particles of physical matter, because these are the A B C's with which Nature has constructed the entire framework of the physical portion of the universe.

The molecule consists of atoms, which are said to be little invisible particles of matter revolving continuously with the speed of lightning, on exactly the same principle that the earth revolves around the sun.

These little particles of matter known as atoms, which revolve in one continuous circuit, in the molecule, are said to be made up of electrons, the smallest particles of physical matter. As already stated, the electron is nothing but two forms of force. The electron is uniform, of but one class, size and nature; thus in a grain of sand or a drop of water the entire principle upon which the whole universe operates is duplicated.

How marvelous! How stupendous! You may gather some slight idea of the magnitude of it all the next time you eat a meal, by remembering that every article of food you eat, the plate on which you eat it, the tableware and the table itself are, in final analysis, but a collection of ELECTRONS.

In the world of physical matter, whether one is looking at the largest star that floats through the heavens or the smallest grain of sand to be found on earth, the object under observation is but an organized collection of molecules, atoms and electrons revolving around one another at inconceivable speed.

Every particle of physical matter is in a continuous state of highly agitated motion. Nothing is ever still, although nearly all physical matter may appear, to the physical eye, to be motionless. There is no "solid" physical matter. The hardest piece of steel is but an organized mass of revolving molecules, atoms and electrons. Moreover, the electrons in a piece of steel are of the same nature, and move at the same rate of speed as the electrons in gold, silver, brass or pewter.

The eighty-odd forms of physical matter appear to be different from one another, and they are different, because they are made up of different combinations of atoms (although the electrons in these atoms are always the same, except that some electrons are positive and some are negative, meaning that some carry a positive charge of electrification while others carry a negative charge).

Through the science of chemistry, matter may be broken up into atoms which are, within themselves, unchangeable. The eighty-odd elements are created through and by reason of combining and changing of the positions of the atoms. To illustrate the modus operandi of chemistry through which this change of atomic position is wrought, in terms of modern science: "Add four electrons (two positive and two negative) to the hydrogen atom, and you have the element lithium; knock out of the lithium atom (composed of three positive and three negative electrons) one positive and one negative electron, and you have one atom of helium (composed of two positive and two negative electrons)."

Thus it may be seen that the eighty-odd physical elements of the universe differ from one another only in the number of electrons composing their atoms, and the number and arrangement of those atoms in the molecules of each element.

As an illustration, an atom of mercury contains eighty positive charges (electrons) in its nucleus, and eighty negative outlying charges (electrons). If the chemist were to expel two of its positive electrons it would instantly become the metal known as platinum. If the chemist could then go a step further and take from it a negative ("planetary") electron, the mercury atom would then have lost two positive electrons and one negative; that is, one positive charge on the whole; hence it would retain seventy-nine positive charges in the nucleus and seventy-nine outlying negative electrons, thereby becoming GOLD!

The formula through which this electronic change might be produced has been the object of diligent search by the alchemists all down the ages, and by the modern chemists of today.

It is a fact known to every chemist that literally tens of thousands of synthetic substances may be composed out of only four kinds of atoms, viz.: hydrogen, oxygen, nitrogen and carbon.

"Differences in the number of electrons in atoms confer upon them qualitative (chemical) differences, though all atoms of any one element are chemically alike. Differences in the number and special arrangement of these atoms (in groups of molecules) constitute both physical and chemical differences in substances, i.e., in compounds. Quite different substances are produced by combinations of precisely the same kinds of atoms, but in different proportions.

"Take from a molecule of certain substances one single atom, and they may be changed from a compound necessary to life and growth into a deadly poison. Phosphorus is an element, and thus contains but one kind of atoms; but some phosphorus is yellow and some is red, varying with the spacial distribution of the atoms in the molecules composing the phosphorus."

It may be stated as a literal truth that the atom is the universal particle with which Nature builds all material forms, from a grain of sand to the largest star that floats through space. The atom is Nature's "building block" out of which she erects an oak tree or a pine, a rock of sandstone or granite, a mouse or an elephant.

Some of the ablest thinkers have reasoned that the earth on which we live, and every material particle on the earth, began with two atoms which attached themselves to each other, and through hundreds of millions of years of flight through space, kept contacting and accumulating other atoms until, step by step, the earth was formed. This, they point out, would account for the various and differing strata of the earth's substances, such as the coal beds, the iron ore deposits, the gold and silver deposits, the copper deposits, etc.

They reason that, as the earth whirled through space, it contacted groups of various kinds of nebulae, or atoms, which it promptly appropriated, through the law of magnetic attraction. There is much to be seen, in the earth's surface composition, to support this theory, although there may be no positive evidence of its soundness.

These facts concerning the smallest analyzable particles of matter have been briefly referred to as a starting point from which we shall undertake to ascertain how to develop and apply the law of POWER.

It has been noticed that all matter is in a constant state of vibration or motion; that the molecule is made up of rapidly moving particles called atoms, which, in turn, are made up of rapidly moving particles called electrons.

THE VIBRATING FLUID OF MATTER: In every particle of matter there is an invisible "fluid" or force which causes the atoms to circle around one another at an inconceivable rate of speed.

This "fluid" is a form of energy which has never been analyzed. Thus far it has baffled the entire scientific world. By many scientists it is believed to be the same energy as that which we call electricity. Others prefer to call it vibration. It is believed by some investigators that the rate of speed with which this force (call it whatever you will) moves determines to a large extent the nature of the outward visible appearance of the physical objects of the universe.

One rate of vibration of this "fluid energy" causes what is known as sound. The human ear can detect only the sound which is produced through from 32,000 to 38,000 vibrations per second.

As the rate of vibrations per second increases above that which we call sound they begin to manifest themselves in the form of heat. Heat begins with about 1,500,000 vibrations per second.

Still higher up the scale vibrations begin to register in the form of light. 3,000,000 vibrations per second create violet light. Above this number vibration sheds ultra-violet rays (which are invisible to the naked eye) and other invisible radiations.

And, still higher up the scale—just how high no one at present seems to know—vibrations create the power with which man THINKS.

It is the belief of the author that the "fluid" portion of all vibration, out of which grow all known forms of energy, is universal in nature; that the "fluid" portion of sound is the same as the "fluid" portion of light, the difference in effect between sound and light being only a difference in rate of vibration, also that the "fluid" portion of thought is exactly the same as that in sound, heat and light, excepting the number of vibrations per second.

Just as there is but one form of physical matter, of which the earth and all the other planets—suns and stars—are composed—the electron—so is there but one form of "fluid" energy, which causes all matter to remain in a constant state of rapid motion.

AIR AND ETHER: The vast space between the suns, moons, stars and other planets of the universe is filled with a form of energy known as ether. It is this author's belief that the "fluid" energy which keeps all particles of matter in motion is the same as the universal "fluid" known as ether which fills all the space of the universe. Within a certain distance of the earth's surface, estimated by some to be about fifty miles, there exists what is called air, which is a gaseous substance composed of oxygen and nitrogen. Air is a conductor of sound vibrations, but a nonconductor of light and the higher vibrations, which are carried by the ether. The ether is a conductor of all vibrations from sound to thought.

Air is a localized substance which performs, in the main, the service of feeding all animal and plant life with oxygen and nitrogen, without which neither could exist. Nitrogen is one of the chief necessities of plant life and oxygen one of the mainstays of animal life. Near the top of very high mountains the air becomes very light, because it contains but little nitrogen, which is the reason why plant life cannot exist there. On the other hand, the "light" air found in high altitudes consists largely of oxygen, which is the chief reason why tubercular patients are sent to high altitudes.

Do not become discouraged if the description of this foundation appears to have none of the thrilling effects of a modern tale of fiction. You are seriously engaged in finding out what are your available powers and how to organize and apply these powers. To complete this discovery successfully you must combine determination, persistency and a well defined DESIRE to gather and organize knowledge.

EVERY MIND BOTH A BROADCASTING AND A RECEIVING STATION

This author has proved, times too numerous to enumerate, to his own satisfaction at least, that every human brain is both a broadcasting and a receiving station for vibrations of thought frequency.

If this theory should turn out to be a fact, and methods of reasonable control should be established, imagine the part it would play in the gathering, classifying and organizing of knowledge. The possibility, much less the probability, of such a reality, staggers the mind of man!

Thomas Paine was one of the great minds of the American Revolutionary Period. To him more, perhaps, than to any other one person, we owe both the beginning and the happy ending of the Revolution, for it was his keen mind that both helped in drawing up the Declaration of Independence and in persuading the signers of that document to translate it into terms of reality.

In speaking of the source of his great storehouse of knowledge, Paine thus described it:

> Any person, who has made observations on the state of progress of the human mind, by observing his own, cannot but have observed that there are two distinct classes of what are called Thoughts: those that we produce in ourselves by reflection and the act of thinking, and those that bolt into the mind of their own accord. I have always made it a rule to treat these voluntary visitors with civility, taking care to examine, as well as I was able, if they were worth entertaining; and it is from them I have acquired almost all the knowledge that I have. As to the learning that any person gains from school education, it serves only like a small capital, to put him in the way of beginning learning for himself afterwards. Every person of learning is finally his own teacher, the reason

for which is, that principles cannot be impressed upon the memory; their place of mental residence is the understanding, and they are never so lasting as when they begin by conception.

In the foregoing words Paine, the great American patriot and philosopher, described an experience which at one time or another is the experience of every person. Who is there so unfortunate as not to have received positive evidence that thoughts and even complete ideas will "pop" into the mind from outside sources?

What means of conveyance is there for such visitors except the ether? Ether fills the boundless space of the universe. It is the medium of conveyance for all known forms of vibration such as sound, light and heat. Why should it not be, also, the medium of conveyance of the vibration of Thought?

Every mind, or brain, is directly connected with every other brain by means of the ether. Every thought released by any brain may be instantly picked up and interpreted by all other brains that are "en rapport" with the sending brain. This author is as sure of this fact as he is that the chemical formula H_2O will produce water. Imagine, if you can, what a part this principle plays in every walk of life.

Nor is the probability of ether being a conveyor of thought from mind to mind the most astounding of its performances. It is the belief of this author that every thought vibration released by any brain is picked up by the ether and kept in motion in circuitous wave lengths corresponding in length to the intensity of the energy used in their release; that these vibrations remain in motion forever; that they are one of the two sources from which thoughts which "pop" into one's mind emanate, the other source being direct and, immediate contact through the ether with the brain releasing the thought vibration.

Thus it will be seen that if this theory is a fact the boundless space of the whole universe is now and will continue to become literally a mental library wherein may be found all the thoughts released by mankind.

This is a lesson on Organized Knowledge. Most of the useful knowledge to which the human race has become heir has been preserved and accurately recorded in Nature's Bible. By turning back the pages of this unalterable Bible man has read the story of; the terrific struggle through and out of which the present civilization has grown. The pages of this Bible are made up of the physical elements of which this earth and the other planets consist, and of the ether which fills all space.

By turning back the pages written on stone and covered near the surface of this earth on which he lives, man has uncovered the bones, skeletons, footprints and other unmistakable evidence of the history of animal life on this earth, planted there for his enlightenment and guidance by the hand of Mother Nature throughout unbelievable periods of time. The evidence is plain and unmistakable. The great stone pages of Nature's Bible found on this earth and the endless pages of that Bible represented by the ether wherein all past human thought has been recorded, constitute an authentic source of communication between the Creator and man. This Bible was begun before man had reached the thinking stage; indeed, before man had reached the amoeba (one-cell animal) stage of development.

This Bible is above and beyond the power of man to alter. Moreover, it tells its story not in the ancient dead languages or hieroglyphics of half savage races, but in universal language which all who have eyes may read. Nature's Bible, from which we have derived all the knowledge that is worth knowing, is one that no man may alter or in any manner tamper with.

The most marvelous discovery yet made by man is that of the recently discovered radio principle, which operates through the aid of ether, an important portion of Nature's Bible. Imagine the ether picking up the ordinary vibration of sound, and transforming that vibration from audio-frequency into radio-frequency, carrying it to a properly attuned receiving station and there transforming it back into its original form of audio-frequency, all in the flash of a second. It should surprise no one that such a force could gather up the vibration of thought and keep that vibration in motion forever.

The established and known fact of instantaneous transmission of sound, through the agency of the ether, by means of the modern radio apparatus, removes the theory of transmission of thought vibration from mind to mind from the possible to the probable.

THE MASTER MIND

We come, now, to the next step in the description of the ways and means by which one may gather, classify and organize useful knowledge, through harmonious alliance of two or more minds, out of which grows a Master Mind.

The term "Master Mind" is abstract, and has no counterpart in the field of known facts, except to a small number of people who have made a careful study of the effect of one mind upon other minds.

This author has searched in vain through all the textbooks and essays available on the subject of the human mind, but nowhere has been found even the slightest reference to the principle here described as the "Master Mind." The term first came to the attention of the author through an interview with Andrew Carnegie.

CHEMISTRY OF THE MIND

It is this author's belief that the mind is made up of the same universal "fluid" energy as that which constitutes the ether which fills the universe. It is a fact as well known to the layman as to the man of scientific investigation, that some minds clash the moment they come in contact with each other, while other minds show a natural affinity for each other. Between the two extremes of natural antagonism and natural affinity growing out of the meeting or contacting of minds there is a wide range of possibility for varying reactions of mind upon mind.

Some minds are so naturally adapted to each other that "love at first sight" is the inevitable outcome of the contact. Who has not known of such an experience? In other cases minds are so antagonistic that violent mutual dislike shows itself at first meeting. These results occur without a word being spoken, and without the slightest signs of any of the usual causes for love and hate acting as a stimulus.

It is quite probable that the "mind" is made up of a fluid or substance or energy, call it what you will, similar to (if not in fact the same substance as) the ether. When two minds come close enough to each other to form a contact, the mixing of the units of this "mind stuff" (let us call it the electrons of the ether) sets up a chemical reaction and starts vibrations which affect the two individuals pleasantly or unpleasantly.

The effect of the meeting of two minds is obvious to even the most casual observer. Every effect must have a cause! What could be more reasonable than to suspect that the cause of the change in mental attitude between two minds which have just come in close contact is none other than the disturbance of the electrons or units of each mind in the process of rearranging themselves in the new field created by the contact?

For the purpose of establishing this lesson upon a sound foundation we have gone a long way toward success by admitting that the meeting or coming in close contact of two minds sets up in each of those minds a certain noticeable "effect" or state of mind quite different from the one existing immediately prior to the contact. While it is desirable it is not essential to know what is the "cause" of this reaction of mind upon mind. That the reaction takes place, in every instance, is a known fact which gives us a starting point from which we may show what is meant by the term "Master Mind."

A Master Mind may be created through the bringing together or blending, in a spirit of perfect harmony, of two or more minds. Out of this harmonious blending the chemistry of the mind creates a third mind which may be appropriated and used by one or all of the individual minds. This Master Mind will remain available as long as the friendly, harmonious alliance between the individual minds exists. It will disintegrate and all evidence of its former existence will disappear the moment the friendly alliance is broken.

This principle of mind chemistry is the basis and cause for practically all the so-called "soul-mate" and "eternal triangle" cases, so many of which unfortunately find their way into the divorce courts and meet with popular ridicule from ignorant and uneducated people who manufacture vulgarity and scandal out of one of the greatest of Nature's laws.

The entire civilized world knows that the first two or three years of association after marriage are often marked by much disagreement, of a more or less petty nature. These are the years of "adjustment." If the marriage survives them it is more than apt to become a permanent alliance. These facts no experienced married person will deny. Again we see the "effect" without understanding the "cause."

While there are other contributing causes, yet, in the main, lack of harmony during these early years of marriage is due to the slowness of the chemistry of the minds in blending harmoniously. Stated differently, the electrons or units of the energy called the mind are often neither extremely friendly nor antagonistic upon first contact; but, through constant association they gradually adapt themselves in harmony, except in rare cases where association has the opposite effect of leading, eventually, to open hostility between these units.

It is a well-known fact that after a man and a woman have lived together for ten to fifteen years they become practically indispensable to each other, even though there may not be the slightest evidence of the state of mind called love. Moreover, this association and relationship sexually not only develops a natural, affinity between the two minds, but it actually causes the two people to take on a similar facial expression' and to resemble each other closely in many other marked ways. Any competent analyst of human nature can easily go into a crowd of strange people and pick out the wife after having been introduced to her husband. The expression of the eyes, the contour of the faces and the tone of the voices of people who have long been associated in marriage, become similar to a marked degree.

So marked is the effect of the chemistry of the human mind that any experienced public speaker may quickly interpret the manner in which his statements are accepted by his audience. Antagonism in the mind of but one person in an audience of one thousand may be readily detected by the speaker who has learned how to "feel" and register the effects of antagonism. Moreover, the public speaker can make these interpretations without observing or in any manner being influenced by the expression on the faces of those in his audience. On account of this fact an audience may cause a speaker to rise to great heights of oratory, or heckle him into failure, without making a sound or denoting a single expression of satisfaction or dissatisfaction through the features of the face.

All "Master Salesmen" know the moment the "psychological time for closing" has arrived; not by what the prospective buyer says, but from the effect of the chemistry of his mind as interpreted or "felt" by the salesman. Words often belie the intentions of those speaking them but a correct interpretation of the chemistry of the mind leaves no loophole for such a possibility. Every able salesman knows that the majority of buyers have the habit of affecting a negative attitude almost to the very climax of a sale.

Every able lawyer has developed a sixth sense whereby he is enabled to "fed" his way through the most artfully selected words of the clever witness who is lying, and correctly interpret that which is in the witness's mind, through the chemistry of the mind. Many lawyers have developed this ability without knowing the real source of it; they possess the technique without the scientific understanding upon which it is based. Many salesmen have done the same thing.

One who is gifted in the art of correctly the chemistry of the minds of others may, figuratively speaking, walk in at the front door of the mansion of a given mind and leisurely explore the entire building, noting all its details, walking out again with a complete picture of the interior of the building, without the owner of the building so much as knowing that he has entertained a visitor. It will be observed, in the lesson Accurate Thinking, that this principle may be put to a very practical use (having reference to the principle of the chemistry of the mind). The principle is referred to merely as an approach to the major principles of this lesson.

Enough has already been stated to introduce the principle of mind chemistry, and to prove, with the aid of the student's own everyday experiences and casual observations that the moment two minds come within close range of each other a noticeable mental change takes place in both, sometimes registering in the nature of antagonism and at other times registering in the nature of friendliness. Every mind has what might be termed an electric field. The nature of this field varies, depending upon the "mood" of the individual mind back of it, and upon the nature of the chemistry of the mind creating the "field."

It is believed by this author that the normal or natural condition of the chemistry of any individual mind is the result of his physical heredity plus the nature of thoughts which have dominated that mind; that every mind is continuously changing to the extent that the individual's philosophy and general habits of thought change the chemistry of his or her mind. These principles the author BELIEVES to be true. That any individual may voluntarily change the chemistry of his or her mind so that it will either attract or repel all with whom it comes in contact is a KNOWN FACT! Stated in another manner, any person may assume a mental attitude which will attract and please others or repel and antagonize them, and this without the aid of words or facial expression or other form of bodily movement or demeanor.

Go back, now, to the definition of a "Master Mind"—a mind which grows out of the blending and co-ordination of two or more minds, IN A SPIRIT OF PERFECT HARMONY, and you will catch the full significance of the word "harmony" as it is here used. Two minds will not blend nor can they be co-ordinated unless the element of perfect harmony is present, wherein lies the secret of success or failure of practically all business and social partnerships.

Every sales manager and every military commander and every leader in any other walk of life understands the necessity of an "esprit de corps"—a spirit of common understanding and co-operation—in the attainment of success. This mass spirit of harmony of purpose is obtained through discipline, voluntary or forced, of such a nature that the individual minds become blended into a "Master Mind," by which is meant that the chemistry of the individual minds is modified in such a manner that these minds blend and function as one.

The methods through whichh this"blen'ing process takes place are as numerous as the individuals engaged in the various forms of leadership. Every leader has his or her own method of co-ordinating the minds of the followers. One will use force. Another uses persuasion. One will play upon the fear of penalties while another plays upon rewards, in order to reduce the individual minds of a given group of people to where they may be blended into a mass mind. The student will not have to search deeply into history of statesmanship, politics, business or finance, to discover the technique employed by the leaders in these fields in the process of blending the minds of individuals into a mass mind.

PRINCIPLE BEHIND MIND CHEMISTRY

The really great leaders of the world, however, have been provided by Nature with a combination of mind chemistry favorable as a nucleus of attraction for other minds. Napoleon was a notable example of a man possessing the magnetic type of mind which had a very decided tendency to attract all minds with which it came in contact. Soldiers followed Napoleon to certain death without flinching, because of the impelling or attracting nature of his personality, and that personality was nothing more nor less than the chemistry of his mind.

No group of minds can be blended into a Master Mind if one of the individuals of that group possesses one of these extremely negative, repellent minds. The negative and positive minds will not blend in the sense here described as a Master Mind. Lack of knowledge of this fact has brought many an otherwise able leader to defeat.

Any able leader who understands this principle of mind chemistry may temporarily blend the minds of practically any group of people, so that it will represent a mass mind, but the composition will disintegrate almost the very moment the leader's presence is removed from the group. The most successful life insurance sales organizations and other sales forces meet once a week, or more often, for the purpose of—OF WHAT?

FOR THE PURPOSE OF MERGING THE INDIVIDUAL MINDS INTO A MASTER MIND WHICH WILL, FOR A LIMITED NUMBER OF' DAYS, SERVE AS A STIMULUS TO THE INDIVIDUAL MINDS!

It may be, and generally is, true that the leaders of these groups do not understand what actually takes place in these meetings, which are usually called "pep meetings." The routine of such meetings is usually given over to talks by the leader and other members of the group, and occasionally from someone outside of the group, meanwhile the minds of the individuals are contacting and recharging one another.

The brain of a human being may be compared to an electric battery in that it will become exhausted or run down, causing the owner of it to feel despondent, discouraged and lacking in "pep." Who is so fortunate as never to have had such a feeling? The human brain, when in this depleted condition, must be recharged, and the manner in which this is done is through contact with a more vital mind or minds. The great leaders understand the necessity of this "recharging" process, and, moreover, they understand how to accomplish this result. THIS KNOWLEDGE IS THE MAIN FEATURE WHICH DISTINGUISHES A LEADER FROM A FOLLOWER!

Fortunate is the person who understands, this principle sufficiently well to keep his or her brain vitalized or "recharged" by periodically contacting it with a more vital mind. Sexual contact is one of the most effective of the stimuli through which a mind may be recharged, providing the contact is intelligently made, between man and woman who have genuine affection for each other. Any other sort of sexual relationship is a devitalizer of the mind. Any competent practitioner of Psycho-therapeutics can "recharge" a brain within a few minutes.

Before passing away from the brief reference made to sexual contact as a means of revitalizing a depleted mind it seems appropriate to call attention to the fact that all of the great leaders, in whatever walks of life they have arisen, have been and are people of highly sexed natures. (The word "sex" is not an indecent word. You'll find it in all the dictionaries.)

There is a growing tendency upon the part of the best informed physicians and other health practitioners, to accept the theory that all diseases begin when the brain of the individual is in a depleted or devitalized state. Stated in another way, it is a known fact that a person who has a perfectly vitalized brain is practically, if not entirely, immune from all manner of disease.

Every intelligent health practitioner, of whatever school or type, knows that "Nature" or the mind cures disease in every instance where a cure is effected. Medicines, faith, laying on of hands, chiropractic, osteopathy and all other forms of outside stimulant are nothing more than artificial aids to NATURE, or, to state it correctly, mere methods of setting the chemistry of the mind into motion to the end that if readjusts the cells and tissues of the body, revitalizes the brain and otherwise causes the human machine to function normally.

The most orthodox practitioner will admit the truth of this statement.

What, then, may be the possibilities of the future developments in the field of mind chemistry?

Through the principle of harmonious blending of minds perfect health may be enjoyed. Through the aid of this same principle sufficient power may be developed to solve the problem of economic pressure which constantly presses upon every individual.

We may judge the future possibilities of mind chemistry by taking inventory of its past achievements, keeping in mind the fact that these achievements have been largely the result of accidental discovery and of chance groupings of minds. We are approaching the time when the professorate of the universities will teach mind chemistry the same as other subjects are now taught. Meanwhile, study and experimentation in connection with this subject open vistas of possibility for the individual student.

POINTS TO REMEMBER

1. The 10 weaknesses that come between you and your goal.
2. Apply the law of the Master Mind in your daily life.
3. The greatest challenge of learning the art of harmonious negotiations with others.

WILL YOU DARE TO EXPLORE THE POWERS OF YOUR MIND?

"You are a mind with a body!"

Because you are a mind, *you* possess mystical powers—powers known and unknown. Dare to explore the powers of your mind! Why explore them?

When you make the discoveries that are awaiting you, they can bring you: (1) physical, mental and moral health, happiness, and wealth; (2) success in your chosen field of endeavor; and even (3) a means to affect, use, control, or harmonize with powers known and unknown.

And dare to investigate all non-physical forces lying outside the realm of known physical processes—forces which you can use when you learn how to apply them. And this will not be so difficult for you—no more difficult than turning on a television set for the first time.

For a little child can tune into his favorite television program. Now, when he does, he neither knows the construction of the broadcasting station or his receiving set, nor the technology involved. But that's all right. For all the child needs to know is how to turn the right knob or push the right button.

You will see in this chapter how you can turn the right knob or push the right button to get what you want from the most effective electrical machine ever conceived. Although this particular machine is the sublime handiwork of Divine Power—you own it. How is it made? Well, among other things, it is comprised of over 80 trillion electrical cells. Naturally, it has many component parts. And each part is in itself an electrical mechanism.

And one part is an electrical marvel. Yet it weighs only fifty ounces. Its mechanism consists of over 10 billion cells which generate, receive, record, and transmit energy.

What is this wonderful machine that you own? Your body. You are and will be the same *you* even though you lose an arm, an eye, or other parts of your body.

And the electrical marvel? *Your brain and your nervous system.* It is the mechanism through which your body is controlled and *through which your mind functions.*

And your mind: it, too, has parts. One is known as the conscious, and the other the subconscious. They synchronize. They work together. Scientists have learned a great deal about the conscious mind. Yet it has been less than a hundred years since we began to explore the vast unknown territory of the subconscious— even though primitive man has deliberately used the mystical powers of the subconscious from the beginning of man's history, and even today the Aborigines of Australia and other primitive peoples do so to a very great extent.

Let's start exploring now!

Day by day in every way I'm getting richer and richer! Let's begin by accompanying Bill McCall of Sydney, Australia on a journey from failure and defeat to success and achievement.

It was at the age of 19 that Bill started a business of his own—hides and skins. He failed. At the age of 21 he ran for Federal Congress. And again he failed. Now it seems that instead of crushing him, these and other defeats motivated this young Australian to develop inspirational dissatisfaction.

So he began searching for rules of success.

You see, Bill McCall wanted to become rich, and he thought

he could find rules for acquiring wealth in inspirational books. Therefore, while checking the inspirational book section of the library, Bill became intrigued by the title *Think and Grow Rich*. He borrowed the book and began to read. He read it once, and then he read it again. And even though he read it the third time, Bill McCall was unable to understand exactly how he could apply the principles whereby some of the richest men in the world acquired their wealth. He told us:

"I was reading *Think and Grow Rich* for the fourth time while walking leisurely along a business street in Sydney. And then it happened! It happened suddenly. I stopped in front of a meat market window and glanced up. And in that very fraction of a second I had a flash of inspiration." He smiled as he continued:

"I exclaimed aloud, 'That's it! I've got it!' I was startled at my emotional outburst. So was a lady who was passing by. She stopped and looked at me in amazement. I hurried home with my new discovery." He continued seriously:

"You see, I was reading Chapter Four entitled *Autosuggestion*. The subheading was *The Medium for Influencing the Subconscious Mind*.

"Now I remember that when I was a boy my father read aloud from Emile Coué's little book *Self-Mastery Through Conscious Autosuggestion.*" He then looked at me and said:

"It was you who pointed out in your book that if Emile Coué was successful in helping individuals avoid sickness and in bringing the sick back to good health, through conscious autosuggestion, autosuggestion could also be used to acquire riches or anything else one might desire. 'Get rich through autosuggestion': that was my great discovery. It was a new concept to me." McCall then described the principles. It almost seemed as if he had memorized them from the book itself.

"You know: conscious autosuggestion is the agency of control through which an individual may voluntarily feed his subconscious mind on thoughts of a creative nature, or, by neglect, permit thoughts of a destructive nature to find their way into the rich garden of his mind.

"When you read aloud twice daily the written statement of your desire for money with emotion and concentrated attention, and you see and feel yourself already in possession of the money, you communicate the object of your desire directly to your subconscious mind. Through repetition of this procedure, you voluntarily create thought habits which are favorable to your efforts to transmute desire into its monetary equivalent.

"Let me say again: It is most important that when you read aloud the statement of your desire through which you are endeavoring to develop a money consciousness, you read with emotion and strong feeling.

"Your ability to use the principles of autosuggestion will depend very largely upon your capacity to concentrate upon a given desire until that desire becomes a burning desire.

"When I arrived home, out of breath for running, I immediately sat down at the dining room table and wrote: 'My definite major aim is to be a millionaire by 1960.'" Still looking at me, he continued, "You mentioned that a person should be specific as to the amount of money he wants and set a date. I did."

Now, the man to whom we were talking was not the young Bill McCall who failed at the age of 19. He became known as the Honorable William V. McCall, the youngest man ever to become a member of the Australian Parliament; as the former chairman of the board of directors of the CocaCola subsidiary in Sydney; and as the director of 22 family-owned corporations. And as to riches—he became a millionaire, and quite as rich as some of the men he had read about in the book from which he got the inspiration *to explore the power of his subconscious mind with self-suggestion.* (Incidentally, he became a millionaire four years ahead of schedule!)

Day by day in every way I am getting better and better! *You will note we use the word "self-suggestion" as being synonymous with the term "conscious autosuggestion" used by Emile Coué.*

McCall remembered that when he was a boy his father had benefited from a great discovery found in a book of his day—a discovery that every man, woman, and child can effectively employ when he finds it for himself. Like Bill McCall and his father, you too can properly employ the power of conscious autosuggestion.

CONSCIOUS SUGGESTION

Now conscious autosuggestion was revealed to Emile Coué because he dared to explore the powers of his own mind and the minds of others. Before he made his great discovery, he used hypnosis to cure the physical illnesses of his patients. But after making his great discovery, which was in reality based on a simple natural law, he abandoned the use of hypnosis.

And how did he find and recognize this natural law?

Emile Coué's great discovery was made when he found the answer to some questions he asked himself. They were:

Question No. 1: Is it the suggestion of the doctor, or is it the suggestion in the mind of the patient, that effects a cure?
Answer: Coué proved conclusively that it was the mind of the patient that subconsciously or consciously made the suggestion to which his own mind and body reacted. Without either *(unconscious) autosuggestion* or *conscious autosuggestion,* external suggestions are not effective.

Question No. 2: If the suggestion of the doctor stimulates internal suggestion of the patient, why can't the patient use healthful, positive suggestions on himself? And why can't he refrain from harmful negative suggestions?

The answer to his second question came quickly: Anyone, even a child, can be taught to develop a positive mental attitude. The method is to repeat positive affirmations such as: *Day by day, in every way, through the grace of God, I am getting better and better.*

Throughout *Success Through a Positive Mental Attitude* you will see many self-motivators which you can use for your own self-suggestion. And if by now you don't know how to use self-suggestion, you will before you complete this book.

When death's door is about to open. There are over 450,000 children born out of wedlock in the United States each year, and over a million and a half teenagers enter penal institutions for car thefts and other crimes. These personal tragedies could in many instances be avoided if: (a) the parents learned how to employ suggestion properly, and (b) if their sons and daughters were taught how effectively to use spiritual self-suggestion. Through the proper use of suggestion, these young people could be motivated to develop inviolable moral standards through their own conscious autosuggestion. And they would know how to neutralize or repel the undesirable suggestions of their associates in an intelligent manner.

Of course, every individual responds to (*unconscious*) autosuggestion throughout his life more often than he does to *conscious* autosuggestion. In such instances he responds to habit and the inner urge of the subconscious. When a man with PMA is faced with a serious personal problem, self-motivators flash from the subconscious to the conscious to aid him. This is especially true in times of emergency—especially when death's door is about to be opened. Such was the case with Ralph Weppner of Toowoomba, Queensland, Australia, one of our PMA Science of Success course students.

It was 1:30 in the morning. In a small hospital bedroom two nursing sisters were keeping vigil beside Ralph's body. At 4:30 the afternoon before an emergency call had been made to his family to rush to the hospital. When they arrived at his bedside, Ralph was in a state of coma as the result of a severe heart attack. The family was now out in the corridor, each one worrying or praying in his own special way.

In the dimly lit bedroom two nursing sisters worked anxiously— one on each wrist—trying to feel a pulse beat. Because Ralph had not come out of the coma during this entire six-hour period and the doctor had done all that he felt he could, the doctor had left the room. He had gone to visit one of his other hospital patients who was also in a critical condition.

Ralph couldn't move, talk, or feel anything. Yet he could hear the voices of the sisters. He could think quite clearly during portions of this period. He heard one sister excitedly state:

"He's not breathing! Can you pick up a beat?"

The answer was, "No."

Again and again he heard the question and answer: "Can you now pick up a beat?" "No."

"I'm all right," he thought, "but I must tell them. Somehow I must tell them."

At the same time he was amused at the sisters for being fooled like that.

He kept thinking, "I'm quite all right. I'm not going to die. But how—how—can I tell them?"

And then he remembered the self-motivator he had learned: *You can do it if you believe you can!*

He tried to open his eyes, but it seemed the more he tried, the more he failed. His eyelids wouldn't respond to the command of his will. He tried to move his arm, his leg, his head—but he couldn't feel any reaction at all. In fact, he didn't feel a thing. Again and again he tried to open his eyes, until at last he heard the words: "I saw one eyelid flicker—he's still there."

"I felt no fear," Ralph says, "and still thought how amusing it was. Periodically one sister called to me, 'Are you there, Mr. Weppner? Are you there?' To which I would try to respond by moving my eyelid to tell them that I was all right—I was still there."

This went on for a considerable time until through constant effort Ralph was at last able to open one, then both, eyes. It was then that his doctor returned. With wonderful skill and persistence the doctor and nurses brought him back to life.

Hidden persuaders. But it was the autosuggestion: *You can do it if you believe you can*—that he had memorized from the PMA Science of Success course—that helped to rescue him when he was at death's door.

THE HIDDEN FORCES

Now the books we read and the thoughts we think affect our subconscious minds. But there are also unseen forces that likewise have powerful effects even though they are subliminal—below the realm of consciousness.

These unseen forces can be from known physical causes or from unknown sources. Before discussing the unknown, let's illustrate with an example that is now common knowledge since the publishing of *Hidden Persuaders* by Vance Packard. The story first appeared in American newspapers and later was picked up in magazines. Let's consider a report that appeared in a leading national magazine on the subject of subliminal advertising. The report tells of an experiment conducted in a New Jersey movie theater, in which advertising messages were flashed on the screen so fast that the viewers were not consciously aware of them.

During a period of six weeks, more than forty thousand persons unknowingly became subjects of this test, while attending the theater. Flashed on the screen by a special process that made them invisible to the naked eye were two advertising messages concerning products that were available in the theater lobby. At the end of the six weeks, results were tabulated: sales of one of the products had soared over 50 per cent, while sales of the other product rose almost 20 per cent.

The inventor of the process explained that, although the messages were invisible, they still had taken effect on many in the audience because of the ability of the subconscious mind to absorb impressions that are too fleeting to be registered consciously.

When this story appeared in the press, the public was horrified "by this attempt to channel our thinking habits, our purchasing decisions, and our thought processes" by the use of subliminal suggestion. People were afraid. They feared brainwashing in its most subtle form. Yet it is amazing to us that someone didn't take the PMA approach. Subliminal suggestion can be employed for desirable objectives, too. Everyone knows that power can be used for evil or for good, depending upon how it is directed.

Now that the experiment has proved its purpose, it doesn't take much imagination to see what the beneficial results to the viewers would be should the following self-motivators be flashed on a movie screen:

God is always a good God!

Day by day, in every way, through the grace of God, you are getting better and better!

Have the courage to face the truth!

What the mind of man can conceive and believe, the mind of man can achieve with PMA!

Every adversity has the seed of an equivalent or greater benefit for those who have positive mental attitude!

You can do it if you believe you can!

This would be a PMA approach, provided, of course, the consent of the audience was obtained in advance.

Another illustration of a known physical force affecting the subconscious mind can be shown by the effect of radar on navigators.

Why did the SS *Andrea Doria* and the SS *Valchem* sink? When the *Andrea Doria*, captained by Pierre Clamai, and the *Stockholm*, under Captain H. O. Nordenson, collided approximately 50 miles off Nantucket Island, 50 persons died.

The *Andrea Doria* was sighted by the radar operator of the *Stockholm* when they were 10 miles apart.

The Grace Line luxury liner, the *Santa Rosa* under Captain Frank S. Siwik, collided with the tanker *Valchem* on March 26, 1959, 22 miles off the New Jersey coast. Four crewmen were killed. Second Mate Walter Wells, the radar operator on the *Santa Rosa,* claimed he had made two plottings of the tanker *Valchem* 's course.

No satisfactory explanation of the true cause of these collisions has resulted from the investigations in either of these instances. Could the waves from the radar instruments have been the real cause? Perhaps Sidney A. Schneider has the answer.

As a young teenager, Sidney A. Schneider of Skokie, Illinois, became interested in hypnotism when he observed his older brother, a university student, successfully place his first subject under hypnosis. Sidney became an expert hypnotist. During his business career he became a radio operator and an engineer in electronics.

In the Second World War Sidney Schneider was a vital part of the system known as "I. F. F."—Information, Friend or Foe. His job was to see to it that every ship leaving our country was equipped with radar. He noticed that radar operators sometimes went into a trance. *They weren't aware that they had been in a trance when they came out of it.*

Because of his knowledge of hypnosis and electronics, Schneider concluded that the fixed attention of the naval employees took place when the waves from the radar machine were synchronized with the brain waves of the operator. On this theory he changed the waves on the radar instrument and eliminated the recurrence of the trances.

Sidney Schneider told us that he converted his conclusions regarding the principle that placed the seamen operating radar in a trance into the Brain Wave Synchronizer, a machine which he invented after the war.

BRAIN WAVE SYNCHRONIZER

What is the Brain Wave Synchronizer?

It is an electronic instrument designed to induce various levels of hypnosis by subliminal and photic (light) stimulation of the brain waves. The instrument can be used alone or combined with a tape recording of the therapist's verbal suggestions. No physical connections or attachments are placed on the patient. Results are obtained at any distance in which the light in the machine is visible. The apparatus induces light to deep hypnotic levels in over 90 per cent of the subjects in an average time of three minutes.

In an experiment with the Brain Wave Synchronizer, none of the persons involved was informed about the machine or what it could do. Neither were they told that they were subjects of an experiment. Yet 30 per cent of them were hypnotized to various degrees, ranging from light to deep states.

"Why and how does the Brain Wave Synchronizer work?" we asked.

"It is like a television transmitter," Schneider said. "The human brain produces pulses (waves) of electricity in several frequency ranges. This knowledge has been applied in the field of medicine since 1929 and the invention of the electroencephalograph commonly known as the EEG machine, an apparatus for recording brain waves.

"My machine operates much like a television system," Schneider continued. "The reason the picture on your receiving set does not drift up or down is that the pulses generated within the set synchronize with corresponding pulses generated by the transmitting television station. The receiver is *forced to operate* at a rate controlled by the transmitter and *the picture must obey.*

"Like the transmitter of a television station, the Brain Wave Synchronizer also produces synchronizing pulses. And through photic stimulation, the waves sent from the synchronizer cause the frequency of the brain waves also to *lock in step*. At this point hypnosis can be achieved. Just compare your brain to a receiving set, and the Brain Wave Synchronizer to a television transmitter."

And you will see as you continue to read that in addition to comparing your brain to a receiving set, you can compare it to a television transmitter also.

A little knowledge becomes a dangerous thing. We have just explored some of the unseen forces from *known physical causes*. Now let's proceed further into the realm of the unknown: the thrilling field of psychic phenomena, such as:

1. ESP (extrasensory perception): awareness of or response to an external event or influence not apprehended by sensory means. Here are included:

    (a) Telepathy: thought transference
    (b) Clairvoyance: the power of discerning objects not present to the senses
    (c) Precognition: seeing into the future
    (d) Postcognition: seeing into the past

2. Psychokinesis: the effect of the mind on an object.

Now let's be realistic and keep our feet firmly on the ground. Let's explore the unknown with common sense! You'll be in danger unless you use good logic and avoid the gathering of cobwebs in your thinking. Facts should be your stepping-stones over the river of doubt. Therefore, let an experienced guide direct you along safe paths. And we will introduce you to such a guide. But before we do, let's talk about the past.

Thomas J. Hudson's famous book, *The Law of Psychic Phenomena,* when published in 1893, became a best seller. (The book is published today in paperback by Kessinger Publishing, White-fish, Montana.) It contained many thrilling stories of reported psychic experiences. The imaginations of tens of thousands of people who read this book were stimulated. Some were ready.

Some were not.

From then on public interest in psychic phenomena made rapid progress. But many persons, not properly prepared, injured themselves by becoming crackpots. This was due to the awesomeness and magnetic interest a little knowledge of psychic powers generated within them. There is a noticeable tendency of some persons who are not properly educated and mature in their thinking and not very well adjusted emotionally to become fascinated with this intriguing study. It is easy to understand why so many religious leaders, scientists, and persons responsible for the welfare of the people found the study of psychic phenomena an anathema:

1. Imaginations ran rampant and threatened the sanity of the people.
2. Fact and fiction seemed to be indistinguishable.
3. Hypnotism by amateurs and vaudeville entertainers, as well as the trickery and frauds practiced by fakirs, mediums, and charlatans abused the minds of the public.
4. Basic religious principles were twisted in a direction that led to evil.

Anything associated with psychic phenomena became repellent. It was taboo.

In spite of the dangers, taboos, and social or professional ostracism, there were courageous, honorable men with good common sense who had the courage to explore for the truth.

But it remained for the long, courageous fight of Dr. Joseph Banks Rhine, formerly of Duke University, inspired and assisted by his wife Dr. Louisa E. Rhine, to clothe the study of psychic phenomena with respectability. This is due to the impeccable character of Dr. Rhine and to his 30 years of *controlled* laboratory experiments based on mathematical laws. His task was a difficult one because spontaneous psychic phenomena are not apt to occur in a laboratory. Such phenomena occur when least expected, and most often when a person is under the greatest emotional strain, or possessed of an intensified obsessional desire—often simultaneously with the death of a loved one.

Westinghouse invests in ESP communication. It is apparent that any writer on the subject of psychic phenomena today endeavors to have the protection of a part of the cloak of Dr. Rhine's respectability by referring to Dr. Rhine and Duke University to make his own theories digestible. We are no exception. We urgently suggest that if you are interested further, you read *The Reach of the Mind* and the other books of which Dr. Rhine is the author or co-author. Our recommendation: Let Dr. Joseph Banks Rhine be your guide.

And how successful has Dr Rhine's work been in breaking down the resistance to investigation and belief in these strange mindpowers? A fair test, it would seem to us, lies in the fact that hard-headed businessmen are convinced and are making experiments of their own. In an interview, Dr. Peter A. Castruccio, Director of the Westinghouse Astronautics Institute, confirmed that Westinghouse scientists are engaged in research to find a means of using telepathy and clairvoyance for long distance communication. Dr. Castruccio too had many lengthy visits with Dr. Rhine before a decision was reached to engage in this great experiment.

And will the search for ways and means to harness telepathy and clairvoyance and make them commercially feasible be successful? Let us answer this as follows: Not too long ago people were scoffing at ideas that were unbelievable to them *then* but are taken for granted *today:* (a) matter being turned into energy and energy into matter; (b) the breaking of the atom; (c) man-made satellites; (d) jet power; or (e) everyday necessities like television, for example.

And what about the electronic computer that was designed from the human computer: the human brain and the nervous system. Every one was conceived, believed, and achieved by men with PMA!

Machines that operate with the speed of light—186,300 miles per second! Machines that can calculate 40,000 arithmetical operations per second and detect and correct their own errors! Machines that became a reality because man built into them electrical circuits which in many respects function like the known electrical activity of the nervous system of your own physical body. Our answer:

What the mind of man can conceive and believe, the mind of man can achieve with PMA!

But no machine or man-made invention is as marvelous as the wonderful human computer you own: your brain and your nervous system, with their power of electrical activity.

Man is more than a body with a brain.

You are a mind with a body—a mind, possessing, and also affected by, powers known and unknown! A mind composed of two parts: the conscious and the subconscious.

POINTS TO REMEMBER

1. Exploring the powers of your mind can bring you long lasting happiness and wealth.
2. It is most important that you read aloud the statement of your desire.
3. The potent effect of unseen forces.

3

IMAGINATION

The imagination is the workshop wherein is fashioned the purpose of the brain and the ideals of the soul. Someone said that, and I don't know of a better definition.

TWO KINDS OF IMAGINATION

There are two forms of imagination. The first one is synthetic imagination, which consists of a combination of recognized old ideas, concepts, plans, or facts that are arranged in a new combination. New things are few and far between. As a matter of fact, when you speak of somebody having created a new idea or anything new, chances are a thousand to one that it's not anything new but merely a reassembling of something that's old that's gone before.

The second form of imagination is the creative imagination. It operates through the sixth sense, has its basis in the subconscious section of the brain, and serves as the medium by which completely new facts or ideas are revealed.

Any new idea, plan, or purpose brought into the conscious mind, which is repeated and supported by emotional feeling, is automatically picked up by the subconscious brain and carried out to its logical conclusion, by whatever natural means are practical and convenient.

I'll repeat part of that statement so you can see a very important point in it—any idea, plan, or purpose that is brought into the conscious mind and is repeated and supported by *emotional feeling*. In other words, ideas in your mind that do not have your emotion, enthusiasm, or faith will seldom produce any action. In order to get action, you've got to get emotion into your thoughts, you've got to have enthusiasm, or you have to have faith.

SYNTHETIC IMAGINATION

Here are some examples of applied synthetic imagination. Let's first consider Edison's invention of the incandescent electric lamp. You may be interested to know there is nothing new about Edison's electric lamp. Both factors that were combined to make up the incandescent light were old and well known to the world long before Edison's time. It remained for Thomas A. Edison to go through ten thousand different failures before he found a way to marry these two old ideas and bring them together in a new combination.

As most of you know, one of these ideas consisted in the fact that you could take and apply electrical energy to a wire, and at the point of friction, the wire would become hot and make a light. A lot of people found that out before Edison's time. Edison's problem was in finding some means of controlling that wire, so that when it was heated to a white heat, it would make a light and it wouldn't burn up.

He tried all of these experiments—ten thousand, to be exact—and none of them worked. Then one day, as he lay down for one of his customary catnaps, he turned the problem over to his subconscious mind, and while he was asleep, the subconscious mind came up with the answer. I've always wondered why it was that he had to go through ten thousand failures before he could get his subconscious mind to act and give him the answer. He already had half of the idea, but after he woke up from that catnap, he knew that the solution to the other half of his problem consisted in the charcoal principle.

To produce charcoal, you put a pile of wood on the ground, set it on fire, then cover it over with dirt, allowing just enough oxygen to percolate through to keep the wood smoldering, but not enough to permit it to blaze. It burns away a certain part of that wood, and the part that's left behind is called charcoal. You know, of course, that where there is no oxygen, there can be no combustion. Taking that concept with which Edison had long been familiar, he went back into the laboratory, took this wire that he had been heating with electricity, put it in a bottle, pumped the oxygen out, and sealed the bottle, cutting off all oxygen, so no oxygen could come in contact with the arc. Then, when he turned on the electrical power, it burned for eight and a half hours. To this day, that's the principle upon which incandescent electric lamps operate. Have you ever noticed that if you drop one of those lightbulbs, it pops like a gun? Do you know why? It does that because all of the air has been drawn out of it. No oxygen is allowed inside that bulb, because if it were, the filament would quickly burn up. That's an example of two old and simple ideas brought together through synthetic imagination.

Examine the operations of your imagination or the imagination of successful people. In a large proportion of the cases, I think you'll find that synthetic imagination, and not creative imagination, was used. The ideas of rearranging old ideas and old concepts can be very profitable.

You may have discovered that there's only one new principle in this philosophy that you're studying (the law of cosmic habit force). In other words, everything here is as old as mankind, and I've only made one contribution that you may not have been familiar with before. What did I do? I used my synthetic imagination and I reassembled existing ideas. In other words, I started out with the salient things that go into the making of success, and I organized them in a way that they had never been organized before in the history of the world. I organized them in a simple form, where you or anyone else can take a hold of them and put them into practical use.

I often wonder why somebody else smarter than I didn't think of that long before I did it. When we get a hold of a good idea, we're always inclined to go back and say, "Why in the world didn't I think of that?" Or, when you do get it, you think, "Why didn't I get it a long time ago, when I needed the money?"

Henry Ford's combination of the horse-drawn buggy and the steam-propelled threshing machine is nothing other than the use of synthetic imagination. He was inspired to create the automobile the first time he saw a threshing machine outfit being pulled along by a steam-propelled engine. There it went down the highway: a threshing outfit with a machine attached to the locomotive of the steam engine. When Mr. Ford observed it, right then and there he got the idea of taking that same principle and putting it onto a buggy (instead of the horse). His "horseless buggy" was eventually known as the automobile.

CREATIVE IMAGINATION

Now let's look at examples of creative imagination. Basically, all new ideas originate through single or mastermind application of creative vision. What does that mean? It generally means that when two or more people get together and begin to think along the same line, in the spirit of harmony (and with the kind of enthusiasm that all the people in the group begin to get when they're working with ideas), out of that group will come an idea pertaining to the thing that they're discussing. In other words, if they go into that discussion for the solution of a major problem, somebody will find the answer, depending on whose subconscious tunes in to the infinite storehouse and picks the answer out first. The answer doesn't always come from the smartest, most brilliant, or best educated man of the group. As a matter of fact, it often comes from the least educated and the least brilliant person in the group.

Let's look at some examples of creative imagination, such as the scientific discovery by Madame Curie. All Madame Curie knew was that, in theory, there must be some radium somewhere in the universe. She hoped it would be on this little ball of mud that we call the earth. See, she had a definite purpose. She had a definite idea. She worked it out mathematically and determined that there was radium somewhere. Nobody had ever seen any, produced any, or found any.

Imagine Madame Curie trying to find radium and compare it to the proverbial story about the person looking for a needle in a haystack. In comparison with her task, I'll take the needle and haystack anytime. By now, I think you might have an idea how she went about searching for it. You don't think she went out with a spade digging in the ground looking for it, do you? Oh no, she didn't do that. She wasn't that foolish.

She conditioned her mind to tune into Infinite Intelligence, and Infinite Intelligence directed her to the source. It's the exact process you use in attracting riches or in attracting anything else you desire. First, you condition your mind with a definite picture of the thing you want. You build it up, and support it with the faith and belief that you're going to get the thing you want, and keep on wanting it even when the going is hard.

The radar and the radio, for example, are by-products of creative imagination and the Wright brothers' flying machine. Nobody had ever created and successfully flown a heavier-than-air machine until the Wright brothers produced theirs. The Wright brothers had no encouragement from the public when they announced that they were going to fly the machine. Until then, they hadn't flown it successfully, but they were going to demonstrate it again at Kitty Hawk, North Carolina. When they announced that to the press, the newspapermen were so skeptical, they wouldn't even go down there. Not one single solitary newspaperman went there for the biggest scoop in the last hundred years. They were smart-alecks, wise guys who knew all the answers. How often does that happen when somebody comes up with a new idea? There are always people who don't believe it can be done because it's never been done before.

There is no limitation to the application of creative vision. The person who can condition his mind to tune in to Infinite Intelligence can come up with the answer to anything that has an answer. Anything, no matter what it is.

Look at Marconi's invention of wireless communication and Edison's talking machine. Before Thomas Edison's time, nobody had ever recorded or reproduced sound of any kind. Nobody ever did that, or anything even resembling it. As far as I know, there hadn't even been any talk about it, or stories written about it, and yet Edison conceived that idea, and almost instantaneously. He took a pencil and a piece of paper or an envelope out of his pocket, and drew a crude sketch of what later became Edison's Incredible Talking Machine, as they called it. It's the one that had a cylinder on it, you know, and when they tried it out, the thing worked the very first time.

It was quite a contrast from his earlier experiences. You see, the law of compensation paid him off for those ten thousand failures, when he thought he was working on the incandescent electric lamp. Don't you see what a generous, and fair, and just thing the law of compensation is? Where you seem to be cheated in one place, you'll find it'll be made up in some other place, in proportion to your efforts, whatever they may be. That works with penalizing, too. Maybe you escape the cop at one corner because you run a red light. Maybe you escape him again, too. But, the next time, he'll catch you on two or three counts. You'll find he eventually catches up with you. Well, somewhere out in nature, there's a tremendous cop and a tremendous recording machine. It records all of our good qualities and all of our bad ones, all of our mistakes and all of our successes. Sooner or later, they all catch up with us.

Let's look at creative vision in evaluating the great American way of life. We still enjoy the greatest privilege of freedom and greatest opportunity for riches mankind has ever known. However, we need to use vision if we are to continue to enjoy these great blessings. If you looked back to see what traits of character have made our country great, here they are. First of all, the leaders who have been responsible for the American way of life made definite application of the seventeen principles of the science of success with emphasis on the following six. At that time, they didn't call these principles by these names, though they were probably conscious that they were applying these principles. One of the strangest things about all of the successful people that I've worked with is that not one of them could sit down and categorically give me a step-by-step modus operandi about how he succeeded. By sheer accident, mind you, they stumbled upon these principles listed here.

In fact, I want you to go back and measure the fifty-six men that signed the Declaration of Independence by these six principles. See if you can trace the application of these principles to their act: 1) Definiteness of purpose, 2) going the extra mile, 3) the mastermind principle, 4) creative vision, 5) applied faith, 6) personal initiative. They made way for the American way of life. They did not expect something for nothing. They did not regulate their working hours by the time clock. They assumed full responsibilities of leadership, even when the going was hard.

Looking back over the past fifty years of creative vision, for instance, we find that Thomas A. Edison, through his creative vision and personal initiative, ushered in the great electrical age. He gave us a source of power the world had not previously known. Think of how one man ushered in a new age—the great electrical age—without which all of this industrial improvement that we've had—all the radar, all the television, all of the radio—would not be possible. What a marvelous thing one person did to influence the trend of civilization all over the world. What a marvelous thing Mr. Ford did when he brought in the automobile. He brought the back woods and Main Street together, he shortened distances, and he improved the value of lands by causing marvelous roads to be built through them. He gave employment directly and indirectly to millions of people who would not have otherwise had employment. Now, millions of people have businesses supplying the automobile trade. Wilbur and Orville Wright changed the size of the earth, so to speak, shortening distances all over the world—just those two men, operating for the good of mankind. Andrew Carnegie, through his creative vision and personal initiative, ushered in the great steel age that revolutionized our entire industrial system and made possible the birth of myriad industries, which could not exist without steel. He was not satisfied with the accumulation of a vast fortune of his own. He raised scores of his associate workers into sizeable fortunes they could not have accumulated without Carnegie's aid. He finished up his life by inspiring the organization of the world's first philosophy of personal achievement, which makes the know-how of success available to the humblest person. What a marvelous thing one man can do, operating through one other man.

When you begin to analyze it, you see what can take place when one individual gets together with another individual and forms a mastermind alliance. They begin to do something useful. There's nothing impossible for two people working together in the spirit of harmony under the mastermind principle. Without that alliance, even if I'd had a hundred lives to live, I could never have created this philosophy. However, the inspiration, faith, confidence, and go-ahead spirit I got by having access to a great man like Mr. Carnegie enabled me to rise up to his level, something I never could have done without this mastermind principle and creative vision. There have been times, if I had listened to what would seem to be logic and reason, I would have quit this philosophy and gotten myself a job, as one of my former relatives said she thought I should have done. I could have gotten a job as a nice bookkeeper somewhere, bringing in seventy-five dollars a week. I'd have been very secure and it would have been wonderful to be at home every night (well, most every night), and everything would have been lovely. Believe you me, I had to fight that argument for quite a while, but I did fight it successfully.

I saw bigger things in life. I began to use not only my synthetic imagination but also my creative imagination (and particularly the latter). It enabled me to pull aside the curtain of discouragement and despair, look into the future, and see there what I now know is taking place all over the world as a result of my having passed this way. All of that through creative vision! How marvelous to be able to tap that thing called creative vision and through it to tune into the powers of the universe. I'm not making a poetic speech, I'm citing science, because everything I'm saying is practical, and is being done, and it can be done by you.

Here is a brief bird's-eye view of what men and women with creative vision and personal initiative have given us. First of all, the automobile, which has practically changed our entire way of living. Those of you who have been born in the last twenty-five, thirty, or even forty years have no concept of what the vibrations of this nation were under the horse and buggy age, in comparison with today. In those days, you would walk down the road, or could ride down the road—safely. Problem is you can't even cross the street where there's a policeman watching in safety, unless you are very alert. The whole method of transportation and the whole method of doing business changed as a result of that one thing called the automobile. Airplanes now travel faster than sound and have shrunk this world to where peoples of all countries know one another better.

Maybe the Creator intended it this way. Instead of these worries and things that we've been having in the past, maybe reducing the world in size would bring the people of all nations within traveling distance, so they would become better acquainted, and finally be neighbors or brothers— under the skin as well as on the skin. If the brotherhood of man ever takes place, it'll be because of these various marvelous things that the imagination of man has uncovered and revealed, bringing us together in ways that make it more convenient for us to assemble and to understand each other all over the world.

You can't carry on a war with a person that you are doing business with each day. You can't fight with the neighbor that you're living by each day and have any peace of mind. Try to get along with the people that you have to come into contact with. You'd be surprised at how many good qualities there are in people you previously didn't like, when you come to know them as they are.

Have you ever considered the radio and television, which give us the news of the world almost as fast as it happens? Without any cost to us, they provide the finest of entertainment to the log cabins of the mountain country and the city mansions alike. It's quite an advance from the days when Lincoln learned to ride on a back of a wooden shovel in a one-room log cabin. It's quite a way from the mountains of Tennessee, and the backcountry of Virginia, where I was born (at that time, only famous for mountain feuds, corn liquor, and rattlesnakes).

You can turn a little knob and tune in the finest operas, the finest music, and the finest everything. You can know what the world is doing almost as fast as it's doing it. You know, if we'd had those conveniences when I was growing up, I doubt if I would have made my first definite major purpose that of becoming a second Jesse James. I probably would have wanted to become a radio operator or something of that sort. My, how all this has changed everything for those mountain people down there, throughout the country, and throughout the world. Just think of all the things the mind of man has brought forth to introduce people to one another.

POINTS TO REMEMBER

1. Ideas in your mind that do not have enthusiasm, or faith will seldom produce any action.
2. Rearranging old ideas and old concepts can be very profitable.
3. The principles that guarantee to help you achieve your ambition.

4

ACCURATE THOUGHT

This is at one and the same time the most *important*, the most *interesting* and the most difficult to present lesson of this entire course on the Law of Success.

It is important because it deals with a principle which runs through the entire course. It is interesting for the same reason. It is difficult to present for the reason that it will carry the average student far beyond the boundary line of his common experiences and into a realm of *thought* in which he is not accustomed to dwell.

Unless you study this lesson with an open mind, you will miss the very keystone to the arch of this course, and without this stone you can never complete your Temple of Success.

This lesson will bring you a conception of *thought* which may carry you far above the level to which you have risen by the evolutionary processes to which you have been subjected in the past; and, for this reason, you should not be disappointed if, at first reading, you do not fully understand it. Most of us *disbelieve* that which we cannot understand, and it is with knowledge of this human tendency in mind that I caution you against closing your mind if you do not grasp all that is in this lesson at the first reading.

For thousands of years men made ships of wood, and of nothing else. They used wood because they believed that it was the only substance that would float; but that was because they had not yet advanced far enough in their *thinking* process to understand the truth that steel will float, and that it is far superior to wood for the building of ships. They did not know that anything could float which was lighter than the amount of water is displaced, and until they learned of this great truth they went on making ships of wood.

Until some twenty-five years ago, most men thought that only the birds could fly, but now we know that man can not only equal the flying of the birds, but he can excel it.

Men did not know, until quite recently, that the great open void known as the air is more alive and more sensitive than anything that is on the earth. They did not know that the spoken word would travel through the ether with the speed of a flash of lightning, without the aid of wires. How could they know this when their minds had not been unfolded sufficiently to enable them to grasp it? The purpose of this lesson is to aid *you* in so unfolding and expanding your mind that you will be able to *think* with accuracy, for this unfoldment will open to you a door that leads to all the power you will need in completing your Temple of Success.

All through the preceding lessons of this course you observed that we have dealt with principles which any one could easily grasp and apply. You will also observe that these principles have been so presented that they lead to *success* as measured by material wealth. This seemed necessary for the reason that to most people the word *success* and the word *money* are synonymous terms. Obviously, the previous lessons of this course were intended for those who look upon worldly things and material wealth as being all that there is to *success*.

Presenting the matter in another way, I was conscious of the fact that the majority of the students of this course would feel disappointed if I pointed out to them a roadway to *success* that leads through other than the doorways of business, and finance, and industry; for it is a matter of common knowledge that most men want success that is spelled SUCCESS!

Very well—let those who are satisfied with this standard of *success* have it; but some there are who will want to go higher up the ladder, in search of *success* which is measured in other than material standards, and it is for their benefit in particular that this and the subsequent lessons of this course are intended.

◆

Accurate thought involves two fundamentals which all who indulge in it must observe. First, to think accurately you must separate *facts* from mere *information*. There is much "information" available to you that is not based upon facts. Second, you must separate *facts* into two classes; namely, the *important* and the *unimportant*, or, the *relevant* and the *irrelevant*.

Only by so doing can you think clearly.

All *facts* which you can use in the attainment of your *definite chief aim* are important and relevant; all that you cannot use are unimportant and irrelevant. It is mainly the neglect of some to make this distinction which accounts for the chasm which separates so widely people who appear to have equal ability, and who have had equal opportunity. Without going outside of your own circle of acquaintances you can point to one or more persons who have had no greater opportunity than you have had, and who appear to have no more, and perhaps less, ability than you, who are achieving far greater success.

And you wonder why!

Search diligently and you will discover that all such people have acquired the habit of combining and using the *important facts* which affect their line of work. Far from working harder than you, they are perhaps working less and with greater ease. By virtue of their having learned the secret of separating the *important facts* from the *unimportant*, they have provided themselves with a sort of fulcrum and lever with which they can move with their little fingers loads that you cannot budge with the entire weight of your body.

The person who forms the habit of directing his attention to the *important facts* out of which he is constructing his Temple of Success, thereby provides himself with a power which may be likened to a trip-hammer which strikes a ten-ton blow as compared to a tack-hammer which strikes a one-pound blow!

If these similes appear to be elementary you must keep in mind the fact that some of the students of this course have not yet developed the capacity to think in more complicated terms, and to try to force them to do so would be the equivalent of leaving them hopelessly behind.

That you may understand the importance of distinguishing between *facts* and mere *information,* study that type of man who is guided entirely by that which he hears; the type who is influenced by all the "whisperings of the winds of gossip"; that accepts, without analysis, all that he reads in the newspapers and judges others by what their enemies and competitors and contemporaries say about them.

THE FACT ABOUT FACTS

Search your circle of acquaintances and pick out one of this type as an example to keep before your mind while we are on this subject. Observe that this man usually begins his conversation with some such term as this—*"I see by the papers,"* or *"they say."* The accurate *thinker* knows that the newspapers are not always accurate in their reports, and he also knows that what "they say" usually carries more falsehood than truth. If you have not risen above the *"I see by the papers,"* and the *"they say"* class, you have still far to go before you become an *accurate thinker.* Of course, much truth and many *facts* travel in the guise of idle gossip and newspaper reports; but the *accurate thinker* will not accept as such all that he sees and hears.

This is a point which I feel impelled to emphasize, for the reason that it constitutes the rocks and reefs on which so many people flounder and go down to defeat in a bottomless ocean of false conclusions.

In the realm of legal procedure, there is a principle which is called the law of *evidence*; and the object of this law is to get at the *facts*. Any judge can proceed with justice to all concerned, if he has the *facts* upon which to base his judgment, but he may play havoc with innocent people if he circumvents the law of *evidence* and reaches a conclusion or judgment that is based upon *hearsay information*.

The law of Evidence varies according to the subject and circumstances with which it is used, but you will not go far wrong if, in the absence of that which you know to be *facts*, you form your judgments on the hypothesis that only that part of the evidence before you which furthers your own interests *without working any hardship on others* is based upon *facts*.

This is a crucial and *important* point in this lesson; therefore, I wish to be sure that you do not pass it by lightly. Many a man mistakes, knowingly or otherwise, expediency for *fact-*, doing a thing, or refraining from doing it, for the sole reason that his action furthers his own interest without consideration as to whether it interferes with the rights of others.

No matter how regrettable, it is true that most thinking of today, far from being *accurate,* is based upon the sole foundation of expediency. It is amazing to the more advanced student of *accurate thought,* how many people there are who are "honest" when it is profitable to them, but find myriads of facts to justify themselves in following a dishonest course when that course seems to be more profitable or advantageous.

No doubt you know people who are like that.

The *accurate thinker* adopts a standard by which he guides himself, and he follows that standard at all times, whether it works always to his immediate advantage, or carries him, now and then, through the fields of disadvantage (as it undoubtedly will).

The *accurate thinker* deals with facts, regardless of how they affect his own interests, for he knows that ultimately this policy will bring him out on top, in full possession of the object of his *definite chief aim* in life. He understands the soundness of the philosophy that the old philosopher, Croesus, had in mind when he said:

"There is a wheel on which the affairs of men revolve, and its mechanism is such that it prevents any man from being *always* fortunate."

The *accurate thinker has* but one standard by which he conducts himself, in his intercourse with his fellow men, and that standard is observed by him as faithfully when it brings him temporary disadvantage as it is when it brings him outstanding advantage; for, being an *accurate thinker*, he knows that, by the law of averages, he will more than regain at some future time that which he loses by applying his standard to his own temporary detriment.

You might as well begin to prepare yourself to understand that it requires the staunchest and most unshakable *character* to become an *accurate thinker*, for you can see that this is where the reasoning of this lesson is leading.

There is a certain amount of temporary penalty attached to *accurate thinking*, there is no denying this fact; but, while this is true, it is also true that the compensating *reward*, in the aggregate, is so overwhelmingly greater that you will gladly pay this penalty.

In searching for *facts* it is often necessary to gather them through the sole source of knowledge and experience of others. It then becomes necessary to examine carefully both the evidence submitted and the person from whom the evidence comes; and when the evidence is of such a nature that it affects the interest of the witness who is giving it, there will be reason to scrutinize it all the more carefully, as witnesses who have an interest in the evidence that they are submitting often yield to the temptation to color and pervert it to protect that interest.

If one man slanders another, his remarks should be accepted, if of any weight at all, with at least a grain of the proverbial salt of caution; for it is a common human tendency for men to find nothing but evil in those whom they do not like. The man who has attained to the degree of *accurate thinking* that enables him to speak of his enemy without exaggerating his faults, and minimizing his virtues, is the exception and not the rule.

Some very able men have not yet risen above this vulgar and self-destructive habit of belittling their enemies, competitors and contemporaries. I wish to bring this common tendency to your attention with all possible emphasis, because it is a tendency that is fatal to *accurate thinking*.

Before you can become an *accurate thinker,* you must understand and make allowance for the fact that the moment a man or a woman begins to assume leadership in any walk of life, the slanderers begin to circulate "rumors" and subtle whisperings reflecting upon his or her character.

NEVER UNDERESTIMATE YOUR OPPONENT

Many a man has gone down to defeat because, due to his prejudice and hatred, he underestimated the virtues of his enemies or competitors. The eyes of the *accurate thinker* see *facts*—not the delusions of prejudice, hate and envy.

An *accurate thinker* must be something of a good sportsman— in that he is fair enough (with himself at least) to look for virtues as well as faults in other people, for it is not without reason to suppose that all men have some of each of these qualities.

"I do not believe that I can afford to deceive others—*I know I cannot afford to deceive myself.*"

This must be the motto of the *accurate thinker.*

◆

With the supposition that these "hints" are sufficient to impress upon your mind the importance of searching for *facts* until you are reasonably sure that you have found them, we will take up the question of organizing, classifying and using these *facts*.

Look, once more, in the circle of your own acquaintances and find a person who appears to accomplish more with less effort than do any of his associates. Study this man and you observe that he is a strategist in that he has learned how to arrange *facts* so that he brings to his aid the Law of Increasing Returns.

The man who *knows* that he is working with *facts* goes at his task with a feeling of *self-confidence* which enables him to refrain from temporizing, hesitating or waiting to make sure of his ground. He knows in advance what the outcome of his efforts will be; therefore, he moves more rapidly and accomplishes more than does the man who must "feel his way" because he is not sure that he is working with *facts*.

The man who has learned of the advantages of searching for *facts* as the foundation of his thinking has gone a very long way toward the development of *accurate thinking,* but the man who has learned how to separate *facts* into the *important* and the *unimportant* has gone still further. The latter may be compared to the man who uses a trip-hammer, and thereby accomplishes at one blow more than the former, who uses a tack-hammer, can accomplish with ten thousand blows.

To make use of *creative thought,* one must work very largely on faith, which is the chief reason why more of us do not indulge in this sort of *thought.* The most ignorant of the race can *think* in terms of deductive reasoning, in connection with matters of a purely physical and material nature, but to go a step higher and *think* in terms of *infinite intelligence* is another question. The average man is totally at sea the moment he gets beyond that which he can comprehend with the aid of his five physical senses of seeing, hearing, feeling, smelling and tasting. *Infinite intelligence* works through none of these agencies and we cannot invoke its aid through any of them.

How, then, may one appropriate the power of *infinite intelligence?* Is but a natural question. And the answer is:

Through creative thought!

THE INFINITENESS OF INTELLECT

To make clear the exact manner in which this is done I will now call your attention to some of the preceding lessons of this course through which you have been prepared to understand the meaning of *creative thought.*

In the second lesson, and to some extent in practically every other lesson that followed it, up to this one, you have observed the frequent introduction of the term "Autosuggestion." (Suggestion that you make to yourself.) We now come back to that term again, because Autosuggestion is the telegraph line, so to speak, over which you may register in your subconscious mind a description or plan of that which you wish to *create* or acquire in physical form.

It is a process you can easily learn to use.

The sub-conscious mind is the intermediary between the conscious *thinking* mind and *infinite intelligence,* and you can invoke the aid of *infinite intelligence* only through the medium of the subconscious mind, by giving it clear instructions as to what you want. Here you become familiar with the psychological reason for a *definite chief aim.*

If you have not already seen the importance of creating a *definite chief aim* as the object of your life-work, you will undoubtedly do so before this lesson shall have been mastered.

Knowing, from my own experience as a beginner in the study of this and related subjects, how little I understood such terms as "Subconscious Mind" and "Autosuggestion" and *"Creative Thought,"* I have taken the liberty, throughout this course, of describing these terms through every conceivable simile and illustration, with the object of making their meaning and the method of their application so clear that no student of this course can possibly fail to understand. This accounts for the repetition of terms which you will observe throughout the course, and at the same time serves as an apology to those students who have already advanced far enough to grasp the meaning of much that the beginner will not understand at first reading.

The subconscious mind has one outstanding characteristic to which I will now direct your attention; namely, *it records the suggestions which you send it through Autosuggestion, and invokes the aid of infinite intelligence in translating these suggestions into their natural physical form, through natural means which are in no way out of the ordinary.* If is important that you understand the foregoing sentence, for, if you fail to understand it, you are likely to fail, also, to understand the importance of the very foundation upon which this entire course is built—*that foundation being the principle of infinite intelligence,* which may be reached and appropriated at will through aid of the law of the "Master Mind" described in the Introductory Lesson.

Study carefully, thoughtfully and with meditation, the entire preceding paragraph.

The subconscious mind has another outstanding characteristic—it accepts and acts upon all suggestions that reach it, whether they are constructive or destructive, and whether they come from the outside or from your own conscious mind.

You can see, therefore, how essential it is for you to observe the law of evidence and carefully follow the principles laid down in the beginning of this lesson, in the selection of that which you will pass on to your sub-conscious mind through Autosuggestion. You can see why one must search diligently for facts, and why one cannot afford to lend a receptive ear to the slanderer and the scandalmonger—for to do so is the equivalent of feeding the subconscious mind with food that is poison and ruinous to creative thought.

The subconscious mind may be likened to the sensitive plate of a camera on which the picture of any object placed before the camera will be recorded. The plate of the camera does not choose the sort of picture to be recorded on it, it records anything which reaches it through the lens. The conscious mind may be likened to the shutter which shuts off the light from the sensitized plate, permitting nothing to reach the plate for record except that which the operator wishes to reach it. The lens of the camera may be likened to Autosuggestion, for it is the medium which carries the image of the object to be registered, to the sensitized plate of the camera. And *infinite intelligence* may be likened to the one who develops the sensitized plate, after a picture has been recorded on it, thus bringing the picture into physical reality.

The ordinary camera is a splendid instrument with which to compare the whole process of *creative thought*. First comes the selection of the object to be exposed before the camera. This represents one's *definite chief aim* in life. Then comes the actual operation of recording a clear outline of that *purpose,* through the lens of Autosuggestion, on the sensitized plate of the subconscious mind. Here *infinite intelligence* steps in and develops the outline of that *purpose* in a physical form appropriate to the nature of the purpose. The part which *you* must play is clear!

You select the picture to be recorded (*definite chief aim*). Then you fix your conscious mind upon this purpose with such intensity that it communicates with the subconscious mind, through Autosuggestion, and registers that picture. You then begin to watch for and to expect manifestations of physical realization of the subject of that picture.

Bear in mind the fact that you do not sit down and wait, nor do you go to bed and sleep, with the expectation of awaking to find that *infinite intelligence* has showered you with the object of your *definite chief aim*. You go right ahead, in the usual way, doing your daily work, *with full faith and confidence that natural ways and means for the attainment of the object of your definite purpose will open to you at the proper time and in a suitable manner.*

The way may not open suddenly, from the first step to the last, but it may open one step at a time.

Therefore, when you are conscious of an opportunity to take the first step, take it without hesitation, and do the same when the second, and the third, and all subsequent steps, essential for the attainment of the object of your *definite chief aim*, are manifested to you.

POINTS TO REMEMBER

1. The two fundamentals of accurate thought.
2. It requires the staunchest and most unshakable *character* to become an *accurate thinker*.
3. There are only rumors of those who are happy and successful.

5

SELECTING A DEFINITE MAJOR AIM AS YOUR LIFE WORK

The mind that has been conditioned to receive attracts that which it needs, just as a magnet attracts steel filings. The most difficult part of any task is getting started. Once a start has been made, however, the ways to complete the job become evident.

The truth of this fact has been proved; people with definite goals achieve far greater success than those who have no goals. And I have yet to find a single successful person who did not readily admit that the major turning point in his life came when he adopted a definite major purpose.

No person can tell another what his or her purpose should be, but once you have adopted your own, you will see how the other principles will come into play and inspire you to action.

Your imagination will become more alert and it will reveal to you many opportunities related to your purpose. Opposition will disappear, and others will give you their friendly cooperation.

Fear and doubt will also disappear, and somewhere along the way you will meet your "other self" face to face—that self which can, and will, carry you to success.

POINTS TO REMEMBER

1. The mind, like a magnet, attracts what it needs.
2. The beginning is the most challenging part of a task.
3. People with definite goals achieve far greater success than those who have no goals.

6

CONTROLLED ATTENTION

I've never known a successful person in the upper brackets of success, no matter what their calling, that hadn't had to acquire great potential powers of concentration in order to achieve their success. I'm talking about highly focused attention upon one thing at a time. You've heard people describe others (intending it to be derogatory, that is) as having "one-track minds," haven't you? Anytime someone says I have a one-track mind, I want to thank him for it, because a lot of people have multitrack minds, and when they try to run on all of them at the same time, they don't make a good job on any of them. Outstanding successes are people who have developed high capacities to keep their mind fixed upon one thing at a time.

When you have learned to concentrate on one thing at a time, you have learned to key yourself up to see yourself already in possession of the thing that you're concentrating on.

CONCENTRATION STARTS WITH A MOTIVE

Motive is the starting point of all concentration, because you don't concentrate unless you have a motive for doing it. Do you want to make a lot of money? Let's say you want to buy an estate, or a farm, and you concentrate on money in the upper brackets. You'd be surprised at how that concentration would change your whole habit and attract to you opportunities for making money that you never thought of before. I know that's the way it works because that's how it worked for me.

Years ago, I wanted a thousand-acre estate. At first, I didn't know just how much a thousand acres was, but I was concentrating on a thousand acres. Actually, the land that I was looking for cost approximately $250,000, which was a lot more money than I had at that time. Nonetheless, from the very day that I fixed my mind on the estate size that I wanted, opportunities began to open up and develop for me to get that money—in larger amounts than I'd ever gotten it before. Royalties on my books commenced to increase, demand for my lectures commenced to increase, and demands for my business counsel commenced to increase. I sold myself on the idea that I had to have the money, and I was going to get it by rendering service for it.

I got the estate. I didn't get a thousand acres, but I got six hundred acres.

I told the man I was buying it from that I wanted a thousand acres. He said, "I have six hundred acres, and by the way, do you know how much six hundred acres are?" I said, "I have a rough idea. Would you mind walking around this estate with me?" We started off bright one morning with a couple of golf sticks we took along to knock the rattlesnakes with. We started around the outer edge, walking up and down the Catskill Mountains, and at noon we weren't even halfway around the property. I said, "Let's just turn around and go back. I've seen enough. Six hundred acres will be plenty." I bought the place and then the Depression came. Believe me, it was tough going but I had accumulated enough money to buy the place. I wouldn't have had it after the Depression, if I hadn't concentrated on that idea.

CONCENTRATION MOTIVATED BY OBSESSIONAL DESIRE

Concentration requires a definiteness of purpose in such proportion that it becomes an obsession. There's no use of having a motive unless you put obsession of desire or obsession of purpose in back of it. What's the difference between an ordinary purpose or desire and an obsessional desire? The word *intensity* is fitting here. In other words, to wish or hope for a thing isn't enough to cause anything to happen. However, when you put a burning desire or obsessional desire back of a thing, why, it moves you into action, attracts you to others, and attracts to you all that you need in order to fulfill that desire.

How do you go about developing an obsessional desire about anything? By thinking about a lot of things, changing from one thing to another? No, you select one thing. You eat it, sleep it, drink it, breathe it, and talk about it to anybody who'll listen. If you can't find anybody, talk to yourself. By repetition, keep telling your subconscious mind exactly what you want. Make it clear, make it plain, make it definite, and, above all else, let your subconscious mind know that you expect results.

INITIATIVE IGNITES CONCENTRATION; APPLIED FAITH SUSTAINS IT

An organized endeavor or personal initiative is the self-starter that begins the action of concentration. Applied faith is the sustaining force that keeps the action going. In other words, without applied faith, when the going gets hard (as it will, no matter what you're doing), you'd either slow down or quit. You need applied faith to keep your action keyed up to a high degree, even when the going is hard and when the results are not coming as you would like them. Have you ever heard of anybody achieving outstanding permanent success right from the start, without any opposition whatsoever? Don't look now, but I'll tip you off—nobody ever did that, and probably nobody ever will. No matter what you're doing, the going is hard for everyone.

There's tremendous amount of information in every one of these lessons that you can concentrate on. You'll have to concentrate on every one of these lessons when you come to it. Put everything else aside and concentrate only on that lesson. Add to your notes everything you can find that's related to the subject, and come back to each lesson many times.

When you do concentrate on any given lesson, don't let your mind run over all the other lessons. Stick to that one lesson while you're at it.

CONCENTRATION OF A MASTERMIND

The mastermind is the source of the live power necessary to ensure success. Can you imagine anybody concentrating on the attainment of something of an outstanding nature without making use of the mastermind, and the brains, and the influence, and the education of other people? Did you ever hear of anybody achieving an outstanding success without the cooperation of other people? I never have and I have been around this success field quite a bit— at least as much as the average and maybe more than the average person—and I have yet to find anyone in the upper brackets of achievement (in any line) that didn't owe his success to the friendly, harmonious cooperation of other people. Their success largely came by means of the use of other people's brains, and sometimes other people's money (because you need to do that once in a while, too). You need the mastermind alliance in your concentration if you're aiming for anything above mediocrity.

Of course, you can concentrate on failure. You won't need any mastermind help on that—although you'll have a lot of volunteer help and a lot of good company if you just aim to fail. But if you're going to succeed, you've got to follow these regulations I'm laying down for you. You can't escape them and you can't neglect any one of them.

SELF-DISCIPLINE

Self-discipline is the watchman that keeps action moving in the right direction, even when the going is difficult. That's when you need self-discipline the most, when you meet with opposition or when the conditions and circumstances that you've got to cut through are difficult. You'll need self-discipline to keep your faith going and keep yourself determined not to quit just because the going is hard. You can't possibly get along in concentrating without self-discipline. If everything went your way, it'd be no trouble at all. You could concentrate on anything if everything was going your way and you didn't meet any difficult circumstances.

IMAGINATION

Creative vision or imagination is the architect that fashions practical plans for your action back of your concentration. Before you can concentrate intelligently, you've got to have plans, you've got to have an architect, and that architect is your imagination (and the imaginations of your mastermind allies, if you have them). What happens when you start out to do something without a definite or practical plan? Have you ever heard of anybody who had a very fine objective, a very fine purpose, or a very fine idea but it failed because he didn't have the right kind of plan for putting it over? Have you ever heard of any other kind except that? It's a common pattern for people to have ideas, but their plans for carrying them out are not good or not sound.

GOING THE EXTRA MILE

Going the extra mile is the principle that ensures harmonious cooperation from others. Going the extra mile is something you need in the business of concentrating. If you're going to get other people to help you, you've got to do something to put them under obligation to you. You've got to give them a motive. Even your mastermind allies in your own organization won't serve as mastermind allies without a motive.

FINANCIAL MOTIVE ENSURES CONCENTRATION

What are some of the motives that would get people to join you in a given undertaking? What's the most outstanding motive? There's financial gain, of course, in all business and professional undertakings. I'd say the desire for professional or financial gain is the most outstanding motive. If you're going into a business where the main object is to make money, and you don't allow your mastermind allies (or the key men and women or the people who are helping you most) to get sufficient returns, you're not going to have them very long. They'll go into business for themselves or they'll go to your competitors.

I was astounded when Andrew Carnegie once told me that he paid Charlie Schwab a salary of $75,000 a year and, in some years, a million-dollar bonus in addition to his salary. He did that for several years. To me, that was a lot of money then, and it's still a lot of money now. It made me curious about Mr. Carnegie. I wanted to know why someone of his great intelligence would pay one man a bonus of more than ten times his salary. I said, "Mr. Carnegie, did you have to do that?" He said, "No, I certainly didn't. I could let him go and be in competition with me. So, no, I didn't have to do it." There's quite a bit of meaning back of that statement. In other words, he had a good man that was very valuable to him, he wanted to keep him, and he knew that the way to keep him was to let him know he'd make more money with Mr. Carnegie than he would without him.

THE GOLDEN RULE

The Golden Rule gives one moral guidance as to the action on which one is concentrating.

ACCURATE THINKING

Accurate thinking prevents daydreaming and focuses on the creation of plans. Do you know that most of the so-called thinking is nothing but daydreaming or hoping or wishing? That's what it is. There are a lot of people in this world who spend the vast majority of their time daydreaming, hoping, wishing, and thinking about things. But they never take any physical or concrete mental action in carrying out their plans.

A long time ago, I was lecturing on this philosophy in Des Moines, Iowa. After the lecture was over, up to the stage toddles an elderly man who was decrepit and not very strong. He fished around in his pocket and brought out a great bundle of papers that had dog-ears on them. He fished among those papers and finally came up with one yellow paper. He said, "Nothing new, Mr. Hill, in what you just said. I had those ideas twenty years ago. Here they are on paper. I had those ideas." Sure he did. Millions of other people had them too, but nobody did anything about them. Nothing new in the philosophy, not a thing new in it, except the law of cosmic habit force. That's the only new thing about it, and strictly speaking, that is not new—that's a proper interpretation of Emerson's essay on compensation, but stated in terms that people can understand the first time they read it. There he was, carrying those ideas around in his pocket. He could have been Napoleon

Hill instead of me, if only he'd gotten busy back before I started. One of these days some smart fellow will come along and take up right where I stop and he'll create the philosophy based on what I've done and perhaps it will be far superior. Maybe that person is here now.

LEARNING FROM DEFEAT AND ADVERSITY

Learning from defeat insures one against quitting when the going is hard. Isn't it a marvelous thing to learn beyond any question of a doubt that failure and defeat and adversity needn't stop you—that there's a benefit in every such experience?

What is the benefit to a man going through a depression, losing all of his money right down to the last penny, and having to start over again? I can tell you, because I am a man who did just that. That was one of the greatest blessings that ever came along, because I was getting just to be a kind of smarty-pants, making too much money, and making it too easily. I had to get taken back a notch. I came out fighting and I've done more good work since that time than I ever did before. Without that experience, I'd probably be up there on my estate in the Catskill Mountains instead of down here teaching.

Sometimes adversity is a blessing in disguise, and often not so disguised, if you take the right attitude toward it. You can't be whipped and you can't be defeated until you have accepted defeat in your own mind. Regardless of the nature of your adversity, there is always a seed of equivalent benefit in it, if you concentrate on the circumstance to look for the good that came of it instead of the bad. Don't spend any time brooding over the things that are lost or gone, or the mistakes that you have made, except to take the time to analyze them, learn from them, and profit by them, so that you won't make the same mistakes twice.

CONTROLLED ATTENTION

Controlled attention involves the blending and the application of many of the other principles of the philosophy. Persistence should be the watchword behind all of these principles.

Controlled attention is the twin brother of definiteness of purpose. Just think what you could do with those two principles, definiteness of purpose —knowing exactly what you want—and concentrating everything you've got on carrying out that purpose. Do you know what would happen to your mind, to your brain, to your own personality, and to yourself if you would concentrate on one definite thing? By concentrating on it, I mean to put all of the time you can possibly spare when you're not sleeping and not working. Devote all of the time that you can possibly spare to see yourself in possession of the thing that represents your definiteness of purpose. See yourself in possession of it, see yourself building plans retaining it, working out the first step you can take, and then the second, and then the third, and so on. Concentrate on it day-in and day-out, and in a little while you'll get to the point where, every way you turn, you'll find an opportunity that will lead you a little bit closer to the thing that represents your definiteness of purpose. When you know what you want, it's astounding how many things you will find that are related to exactly what you want.

When I was living in Florida several years ago, I had a very important letter coming to the Tampa, Florida, Post Office. I knew the letter came because I talked to the National City Bank in New York. I knew that letter was in the mail and was down at the post office—and I had to have it before twelve o'clock. I called the postmaster, who was a friend of mine, and he said, "That mail is somewhere between here and your Temple Parish (which was ten miles away, since I lived out in the country). It's on Route 1 and I don't know any way you can get that letter before twelve o'clock unless you run that postman down. I'll tell you which stations to start at, because he's already passed station number nine. If you want to pick him up there, I'll give you the instructions on how to follow his route."

Well, Route 1 was the same highway I used to travel from Tampa to my home in Temple Parish. I traveled that highway every day. I didn't know there were any mailboxes on it but when it began to be important for me to observe mailboxes, I never saw so many mailboxes in all my life. Believe me, there looked to be a mailbox almost every hundred feet! They were all numbered and I was looking for the number the postmaster had given me as the one where he would probably be at that very hour and I finally caught up with him. It was on a Monday, and so he had an enormous load of mail. He said, "Man, I can't do anything about it. I don't know where your letter is and I won't know until I get rid of all this mail." I said, "Listen, fellow, I have got to have that letter. It's in there, and I have got to have it. The postmaster told me to run you down and not to take no for an answer. He said to tell you to get out and sort that mail and let me have that letter. That's what he told me, and if you don't think so, come right over here to this farmhouse and call him yourself." He said, "I can't do that. It's unlawful." I said, "Unlawful or not, I've got to have that letter now and that's all there is to it. Now listen, fellow, be a good sport. No use you and me arguing. You've got a job to do and I've got a job to do. Mine's important and yours is important. It's not going to hurt you very much to go through that mail." "Oh, hell," he said, "all right." So he went to work and the third letter that he picked out was mine. The third one. It's just one of those things, when you know what you want, somehow or other you're determined to get it, and it's not nearly as difficult to get as you thought it would be.

I often think of that experience, how indicative it is of people who know what they want and are successful in getting it. They don't let anything stop them at all. They don't pay any attention to opposition.

I've often watched my distinguished business associate, Mr. Stone, talk to his salesmen. I get a thrill every time I hear him speak, because I don't believe he knows what the word *no* means. I think he's long since believed it means yes—and the results he gets show that he believes it means yes. He can be the most definite about the things he wants of anybody I've ever known. He's the most definite about failure and in refusing to accept a turndown. When objects get in his way, he just moves right over them, around them, or blows them out of the way, but he never lets them stop him.

That's concentration and definiteness of purpose put into action.

Everybody knows what Henry Ford's definiteness of purpose was. People have been riding around in a part of his major purpose every day of their lives. It was a low-price, dependable automobile. He didn't allow anybody to talk him out of it. I have heard promoters approach Mr. Ford with opportunities that seem to me most glittering. He told them that the thing he was engaged in consumed all of his time and all his effort. He was not interested in anything outside of his definite major purpose, which was to make and distribute all over the world low-priced, dependable automobiles. Sticking to that job made him fabulously rich.

I saw hundreds of people spend infinitely more money than Mr. Ford had when he started out, and they ended up in the graveyard of failure. I couldn't find a dozen people in the world today who would know what their names were. Men who were better educated than Mr. Ford, had better personalities, and had everything that he had and a lot more, except one thing. They didn't stick to the one definiteness of purpose the way he did when the going was hard.

As an inventor, Mr. Edison gives a marvelous illustration of what concentration can do. Truth be known, Mr. Edison was a genius in any sense, because when the going was hard, that's when he turned on the most steam and didn't quit. Think of a man keeping on through ten thousand different failures as he did when he was working on the incandescent electric lamp. Ten thousand! Can you imagine going through ten thousand failures in the same field without wondering if you shouldn't have your head examined? I was astounded when I heard that and actually saw his logbooks. There were two logbooks, each with about two hundred and fifty pages, and on every page there was a different plan that he had tried, which failed. I said, "Mr. Edison, suppose that you hadn't found the answer. What would you be doing right now?" He said, "I would be in my laboratory working instead of out here fooling away my time with you." He grinned when he said it, but he meant exactly what he was saying.

INFINITE INTELLIGENCE ON YOUR SIDE

If you don't give up when the going is hard, Infinite Intelligence will throw itself on your side. You will have your faith, your initiative, your enthusiasm, and your endurance tested, but when nature finds out that you can stand the test, and you're not going to take no for an answer, it will say, "You pass. You're in."

I think that nature—or Infinite Intelligence, or God, first cause, or whatever you choose to call it—conveys information to people in simple terms, in ways they can understand. That's what this philosophy teaches. It's not like sending a high school boy or girl to the dictionary or to the encyclopedia to read about it. On the contrary, you *understand* it. Your own intelligence tells you the moment you come across one of these principles that it's sound. You don't need any proof; you can see that it's sound. This philosophy wouldn't be in existence today if I hadn't concentrated on it through twenty-odd years of adversity and defeat. It pays to concentrate and my own experience corroborates this—if you stand by when the going is hard, Infinite Intelligence will throw itself on your side.

I don't think that would be true in a case like that of Hitler's. No doubt he had definiteness of purpose and an obsessional desire. What was wrong with his definiteness of purpose is that it ran counter to the plans of Infinite Intelligence, the laws of nature, and the laws of right and wrong.

You may be sure that whatever you're doing will come to naught, to failure, and to grief if it works a hardship or an injustice upon a single individual. If you hope to have Infinite Intelligence throw itself on your side, you must be "right," meaning that everything you do benefits everybody whom it affects, including yourself.

Christ's whole life was devoted to concentration upon a system of living for the brotherhood of man. He didn't fare too well while he lived, but he must have been doing the right thing, because if it hadn't been right, it would have been destroyed and gone long before this. He may have only had twelve people to start but I believe what he was preaching must have been right based on what's happened since he passed on.

There is something in nature (or in Infinite Intelligence), which brings forth with every evil the virus of its own destruction. There's no exception to that. The overall plan of nature and the natural laws of the universe dictate that, no matter what the circumstance, every evil, by itself, brings its own virus of its own destruction.

Take William Wrigley for instance. William Wrigley Jr. was the first man that ever paid me for teaching this philosophy. My first hundred dollars that I ever made came from William Wrigley. Just think what that man did on a five-cent package of chewing gum. I never ride down Michigan Boulevard and see that building on the river, lit up at night, that I don't think of what concentration can do even with such a thing as a five-cent package of chewing gum.

The signers of the Declaration of Independence, George Washington, Abraham Lincoln, and Thomas Jefferson had the concentration to give personal liberties to all of the American people and, eventually, to the people of the world. It may well be that

America is the cradle for the birth of freedom of mankind. I know of no other nation on the face of this earth that is concentrating upon the freedom of the individual as we're doing here in the United States. I know of no other philosophy, and no one as engaged in any other study, whose objective is to free so many people as those who are studying this philosophy.

POINTS TO REMEMBER

1. Learn to concentrate on one thing at a time.
2. Personal initiative is the self-starter that begins the action of concentration.
3. The requirement of self-discipline to keep yourself from not quitting.

7

ENTHUSIASM

Enthusiasm is a state of mind that inspires and arouses one to put *action* into the task at hand. It does more than this—it is contagious, and vitally affects not only the enthusiast, but all with whom he comes in contact.

Enthusiasm bears the same relationship to a human being that steam does to the locomotive—it is the vital moving force that impels *action*. The greatest leaders of men are those who know how to inspire enthusiasm in their followers. Enthusiasm is the most important factor entering into salesmanship. It is, by far, the most vital factor that enters into public speaking.

If you wish to understand the difference between a man who is enthusiastic and one who is not, compare Billy Sunday with the average man of his profession. The finest sermon ever delivered would fall upon deaf ears if it were not backed with enthusiasm by the speaker.

HOW ENTHUSIASM WILL AFFECT YOU

Mix enthusiasm with your work and it will not seem hard or monotonous. Enthusiasm will so energize your entire body that you can get along with less than half the usual amount of sleep and at the same time it will enable you to perform from two to three times as much work as you usually perform in a given period, without fatigue.

For many years I have done most of my writing at night. One night, while I was enthusiastically at work over my typewriter, I looked out of the window of my study, just across the square from the Metropolitan tower, in New York City, and saw what seemed to be the most peculiar reflection of the moon on the tower. It was of a silvery gray shade, such as I had never seen before. Upon closer inspection I found that the reflection was that of the early morning sun and not that of the moon. It was daylight! I had been at work all night, but I was so engrossed in my work that the night had passed as though it were but an hour. I worked at my task all that day and all the following night without stopping, except for a small amount of light food.

Two nights and one day without sleep, and with but little food, without the slightest evidence of fatigue, would not have been possible had I not kept my body energized with *enthusiasm* over the work at hand.

Enthusiasm is not merely a figure of speech; it is a vital force that you can harness and use with profit. Without it you would resemble an electric battery without electricity.

Enthusiasm is the vital force with which you recharge your body and develop a dynamic personality. Some people are blessed with natural *enthusiasm*, while others must acquire it. The procedure through which it may be developed is simple. It begins by the doing of the work or rendering of the service which one likes best. If you should be so situated that you cannot conveniently engage in the work which you like best, for the time being, then you can proceed along another line very effectively by adopting a *definite chief aim* that contemplates your engaging in that particular work at some future time.

Lack of capital and many other circumstances over which you have no immediate control may force you to engage in work which you do not like, but no one can stop you from determining in your own mind what your *definite chief aim* in life shall be, nor can anyone stop you from planning ways and means for translating this aim into reality, nor can anyone stop you from mixing *enthusiasm* with your plans.

Happiness, the final object of all human effort, is a state of mind that can be maintained only through the hope of future achievement. Happiness lies always in the future and never in the past. The happy person is the one who dreams of heights of achievement that are yet unattained. The home you intend to own, the money you intend to earn and place in the bank, the trip you intend to take when you can afford it, the Position in life you intend to fill when you have prepared yourself, and the preparation, itself—these are the things that produce happiness. Likewise, these are the materials out of which your *definite chief aim* is formed; these are the things over which you may become *enthusiastic*, no matter what your present station in life may be.

More than twenty years ago I became enthusiastic over an idea. When the idea first took form in my mind I was unprepared to take even the first step toward its transformation into reality. But I nursed it in my mind—I became *enthusiastic* over it as I looked ahead, in my imagination, and saw the time when I would be prepared to make it a reality.

The idea was this: I wanted to become the editor of a magazine, based upon the Golden Rule, through which I could inspire people to keep up courage and deal with one another squarely.

Finally my chance came! and, on armistice day, 1918, I wrote the first editorial for what was to become the material realization of a hope that had lain dormant in my mind for nearly a score of years.

With *enthusiasm* I poured into that editorial the emotions which I had been developing in my heart over a period of more than twenty years. My dream had come true. My editorship of a national magazine had become a reality.

As I have stated, this editorial was written with *enthusiasm*. I took it to a man of my acquaintance and with *enthusiasm* I read it to him. The editorial ended in these words: "At last my twenty-year-old dream is about to come true. It takes money, and a lot of it, to publish a national magazine, and I haven't the slightest idea where I am going to get this essential factor, but this is worrying me not at all because *I know I am going to get it somewhere!*" As I wrote those lines, I mixed *enthusiasm* and faith with them.

I had hardly finished reading this editorial when the man to whom I read it—the first and only person to whom I had shown it—said:

"I can tell you where you are going to get the money, for I am going to supply it." And he did!

Yes, *enthusiasm* is a vital force; so vital, in fact, that no man who has it highly developed can begin even to approximate his power of achievement.

Before passing to the next step in this lesson, I wish to repeat and to emphasize the fact that you may develop *enthusiasm* over your *definite chief aim* in life, no matter whether you are in position to achieve that purpose at this time or not. You may be a long way from realization of your *definite chief aim,* but if you will kindle the fire of *enthusiasm* in your heart, and keep it burning, before very long the obstacles that now stand in the way of your attainment of that purpose will melt away as if by the force of magic, and you will find yourself in possession of power that you did not know you possessed.

HOW YOUR ENTHUSIASM WILL AFFECT OTHERS

We come, now, to the discussion of one of the most important subjects of this Reading Course, namely, *suggestion.*

In the preceding lessons we have discussed the subject of *Autosuggestion,* which is self-suggestion.

Suggestion is the principle through which your words and

your acts and even *your state of mind* influence others. That you may comprehend the far-reaching power of *suggestion,* let me refer to the Introductory Lesson, in which the principle of telepathy is described. If you now understand and accept the principle of telepathy (the communication of thought from one mind to another without the aid of signs, symbols or sounds) as a reality, you of course understand why *enthusiasm* is contagious, and why it influences all within its radius.

When your own mind is vibrating at a high rate, because it has been stimulated with *enthusiasm,* that vibration registers in the minds of all within its radius, and especially in the minds of those with whom you come in close contact. When a public speaker "senses" the feeling that his audience is "en rapport" with him he merely recognizes the fact that his own *enthusiasm* has influenced the minds of his listeners until their minds are vibrating in harmony with his own.

When the salesman "senses" the fact that the "psychological" moment for closing a sale has arrived, he merely feels the effect of his own *enthusiasm* as it influences the mind of his prospective buyer and places that mind "en rapport" (in harmony) with his own.

The subject of *suggestion* constitutes so vitally an important part of this lesson, and of this entire course, that I will now proceed to describe the three mediums through which it usually operates; namely, what you say, what you do and what you *think!*

When you are enthusiastic over the goods you are selling or the services you are offering, or the speech you are delivering, your state of mind becomes obvious to all who hear you, *by the tone of your voice.*

Whether you have ever thought of it in this way or not, it is the tone in which you make a statement, more than it is the statement itself, that carries conviction or fails to convince. No mere combination of words can ever take the place of a deep belief in a statement that is expressed with burning *enthusiasm*. Words are but devitalized sounds unless colored with feeling that is born of *enthusiasm*.

Here the printed word fails me, for I can never express with mere type and paper the difference between words that fall from unemotional lips, without the fire of *enthusiasm* hack of them, and those which seem to pour forth from a heart that is bursting with eagerness for expression. The difference is there, however.

Thus, *what you say*, and the way in which you say it, conveys a meaning that may be just the opposite to what is intended. This accounts for many a failure by the salesman who presents his arguments in words which seem logical enough, but lack the coloring that can come only from *enthusiasm* that is born of sincerity and belief in the goods he is trying to sell. His, words said one thing, but the tone of his voice *suggested* something entirely different; therefore, no sale was made.

That which you *say* is an important factor in the operation of the principle of *suggestion,* but not nearly so important as that which you *do. Your acts will count for more than your words,* and woe unto you if the two fail to harmonize.

If a man preach the Golden Rule as a sound rule of conduct his words will fall upon deaf ears if he does not practice that which he preaches. The most effective sermon that any man can preach on the soundness of the Golden Rule is that which he preaches, by *suggestion,* when he applies this rule in his relationships with his fellow men.

If a salesman of Ford automobiles drives up to his prospective purchaser in a Buick, or some other make of car, all the arguments he can present in behalf of the Ford will be without effect. Once I went into one of the offices of the Dictaphone Company to look at a Dictaphone (dictating machine). The salesman in charge presented a logical argument as to the machine's merits, while the stenographer at his side was transcribing letters from a shorthand notebook. His arguments in favor of a dictating machine, as compared with the old method of dictating to a stenographer, did not impress me, because his actions were not in harmony with his words.

Your *thoughts* constitute the most important of the three ways in which you apply the principle of *suggestion,* for the reason that they control the tone of your words and, to some extent at least, your actions. If your *thoughts* and your *actions* and your *words* harmonize, you are bound to influence those with whom you come in contact, more or less toward your way of thinking.

We will now proceed to analyze the subject of *suggestion* and to show you exactly how to apply the principle upon which it operates. As we have already seen, *suggestion* differs from Autosuggestion only in one way—we use it, consciously or unconsciously, when we influence others, while we use *Autosuggestion* as a means of influencing ourselves.

Before you can influence another person through *suggestion,* that person's mind must be in a state of neutrality; that is, it must be open and receptive to your method of *suggestion.* Right here is where most salesmen fail—they try to make a sale before the mind of the prospective buyer has been rendered receptive or neutralized. This is such a vital point in this lesson that I feel impelled to dwell upon it until there can be no doubt that you understand the principle that I am describing.

When I say that the salesman must neutralize the mind of his prospective purchaser before a sale can be made I mean that the prospective purchaser's mind must be credulous. A state of confidence must have been established and it is obvious that there can be no set rule for either establishing confidence or neutralizing the mind to a state of openness. Here the ingenuity of the salesman must supply that which cannot be set down as a hard and fast rule.

I know a life insurance salesman who sells nothing but large policies, amounting to $100,000.00 and upward. Before this man even approaches the subject of insurance with a prospective client he familiarizes himself with the prospective client's complete history, including his education, his financial status, his eccentricities if he has any, his religious preferences and other data too numerous to be listed. Armed with this information, he manages to secure an introduction under conditions which permit him to know the Prospective client in a social as well as a business way. Nothing is said about the sale of life insurance during his first visit, nor his second, and sometimes he does not approach the subject of insurance until he has become very well acquainted with the prospective client.

All this time, however, he is not dissipating his efforts. He is taking advantage of these friendly visits for the purpose of neutralizing his prospective client's mind; that is, he is building up a relationship of confidence so that when the time comes for him to talk life insurance that which he says will fall upon ears that *willingly listen.*

Some years ago I wrote a book entitled *How to Sell Your Services.* Just before the manuscript went to the publisher, it occurred to me to request some of the well-known men of the United States to write letters of endorsement to be published in the book. The printer was then waiting for the manuscript; therefore, I hurriedly wrote a letter to some eight or ten men, in which l briefly outlined exactly what I wanted, but the letter brought back no replies. I had failed to observe two important prerequisites for success—I had written the letter so hurriedly that I had failed to inject the spirit of *enthusiasm* into it, and, I had neglected so to word the letter that it had the effect of neutralizing the minds of those to whom it was sent; therefore, I had not paved the way for the application of the principle of *suggestion.*

After I discovered my mistake, I then wrote a letter that was based upon strict application of the principle of *suggestion,* and this letter not only brought back replies from all to whom it was sent, but many of the replies were masterpieces and served, far beyond my fondest hopes, as valuable supplements to the book.

NOT ALL ADVICE IS GOOD ADVICE

Suggestion is one of the most subtle and powerful principles of psychology. You are making use of it in all that you do and say and think, but, unless you understand the difference between negative suggestion and positive suggestion, you may be using it in such a way that it is bringing you defeat instead of success.

Science has established the fact that through the negative use of suggestion life may be extinguished. Some years ago, in France, a criminal was condemned to death, but before the time for his execution an experiment was performed on him which conclusively proved that through the principle of suggestion, death could be produced. The criminal was brought to the guillotine and his head was placed under the knife, after he had been blindfolded. A heavy, sharp edged plank was then dropped on his neck, producing a shock similar to that of a sharp edged knife. Warm water was then gently poured on his neck and allowed to trickle slowly down his spine, to imitate the flow of warm blood. In seven minutes the doctors pronounced the man dead. His imagination, through the principle of suggestion, had actually turned the sharp edged plank into a guillotine blade and stopped his heart from beating.

In the little town where I was raised, there lived an old lady who constantly complained that she feared death from cancer. During her childhood she had seen a woman who had cancer and the sight had so impressed itself upon her mind that she began to look for the symptoms of cancer in her own body. She was sure that every little ache and pain was the beginning of her long-looked-for symptom of cancer. I have seen her place her hand on her breast and have heard her exclaim, "Oh, I am sure I have a cancer growing here. I can feel it." When complaining of this imaginary disease, she always placed her hand on her left breast, where she believed the cancer was attacking her.

For more than twenty years she kept this up.

A few weeks ago she died—*with cancer on her left breast!* If suggestion will actually turn the edge of a plank into a guillotine blade and transform healthy body cells into parasites out of which cancer will develop, can you not imagine what it will do in destroying disease germs, if properly directed? *Suggestion* is the law through which mental healers work what appear to be miracles. I have personally witnessed the removal of parasitical growths known as warts, through the aid of suggestion, within forty-eight hours.

You—the reader of this lesson—can be sent to bed with *imaginary* sickness of the worst sort, in two hours' time or less, through the use of *suggestion.* If you should start down the street and three or four people in whom you had confidence should meet you and each exclaim that you look ill you would be ready for a doctor.

I wish to take advantage of this appropriate opportunity to state that all of the really big men whom I have had the pleasure of knowing have been the most willing and courteous men of my acquaintance when it came to rendering service that was of benefit to others. Perhaps that was one reason why they were *really* big men.

THE HUMAN MIND IS A MARVELOUS PIECE OF MACHINERY!

One of its outstanding characteristics is noticed in the fact that all impressions which reach it, either through outside *suggestion* or Autosuggestion, are recorded together in groups which harmonize in nature. The negative impressions are stored away, all in one portion of the brain, while the positive impressions are stored in another portion. When one of these impressions (or past experiences) is called into the conscious mind, through the principle of memory, there is a tendency to recall with it all others of a similar nature, just as the raising of one link of a chain brings up other links with it. For example, anything that causes a feeling of doubt to arise in a person's mind is sufficient to call forth all of his experiences which caused him to become doubtful. If a man is asked by a stranger to cash a check, immediately he remembers having cashed checks that were not good, or of having heard of others who did so. Through the law of association all similar emotions, experiences and sense impressions that reach the mind are filed away together, so that the recalling of one has a tendency to bring back to memory all the others.

To arouse a feeling of distrust in a person's mind has a tendency to bring to the surface every doubt-building experience that person ever had. For this reason successful salesmen endeavor to keep away from the discussion of subjects that may arouse the buyer's "chain of doubt impressions" which he has stored away by reason of previous experiences. The successful salesman quickly learns that "knocking" a competitor or a competing article may result in bringing to the buyer's mind certain negative emotions growing out of previous experiences which may make it impossible for the salesman to "neutralize" the buyer's mind.

This principle applies to and controls every sense impression that is lodged in the human mind. Take the feeling of fear, for example; the moment we permit a single emotion that is related to fear to reach the conscious mind, it calls with it all of its unsavory relations. A feeling of courage cannot claim the attention of the conscious mind while a feeling of fear is there. One or the other must dominate. They make poor roommates because they do not harmonize in nature. Like attracts like. Every thought held in the conscious mind has a tendency to draw to it other thoughts of a similar nature. You see, therefore, that these feelings, thoughts and emotions growing out of past experiences, which claim the attention of the conscious mind, are backed by a regular army of supporting soldiers of a similar nature, that stand ready to aid them in their work.

Deliberately place in your own mind, through the principle of Autosuggestion, the ambition to succeed through the aid of a *definite chief aim,* and notice how quickly all of your latent or undeveloped ability in the nature of past experiences will become stimulated and aroused to action in your behalf. Plant in a boy's mind, through the principle of *suggestion,* the ambition to become a successful lawyer or doctor or engineer or business man or financier, and if you plant that suggestion deeply enough, and keep it there, by repetition, it will begin to move that boy toward the achievement of the object of that ambition.

If you would plant a *suggestion* "deeply," mix it generously with *enthusiasm,* for enthusiasm is the fertilizer that will insure its rapid growth as well as its permanency.

When that kind-hearted old gentleman planted in my mind the suggestion that I was a "bright boy" and that I could make my mark in the world if I would educate myself, it was not so much *what* he said, as it was the *way in which he said it* that made such a deep and lasting impression on my mind. It was the way in which he gripped my shoulders and the look of confidence in his eyes that drove his suggestion so deeply into my subconscious mind that it never gave me any peace until I commenced taking the steps that led to the fulfillment of the suggestion.

This is a point that I would stress with all the power at my command. *It is not so much what you say as it is the TONE and MANNER in which you say it that makes, a lasting impression.*

It naturally follows, therefore, that sincerity of purpose, honesty and earnestness must be placed back of all that one says if one would make a lasting and favorable impression.

Whatever you successfully sell to others you must first sell to *yourself.*

POINTS TO REMEMBER

1. Enthusiasm is the vital moving force that impels *action*.
2. Thoughts can be influenced through suggestion and autosuggestion.
3. Happiness is the final object of all human effort.

8

KNOW YOUR MIND,
LIVE YOUR OWN LIFE

You have a great potential for success, but first you must know your own mind and live your own life—then you will find and enjoy that mighty potential. Become acquainted with your inner self and you can win what you want within a time limit of your own choosing. Certain special techniques help you win the goals of your dearest dreams, and every one of these techniques is easily within your power.

SOMEWHERE along the path of life, every successful man finds out how to live his own life as he wishes to live it.

The younger you are when you discover this mighty power, the more likely you are to live successfully and happily. Yet even in later years, many make the great change—from letting others make them what they are, to making sure that they make their lives to their own liking.

The Creator gave man the prerogative of power over his own mind. It must have been the Creator's purpose to encourage man to live his own life, think his own thoughts, find his own goals and achieve them. Simply by exercising this profound prerogative you can bring abundance into your life, and with it know the greatest wealth of all, peace of mind, without which there can be no real happiness.

You live in a world filled with outside influences which impinge upon you. You are influenced by other people's acts and wishes, by law and custom, by your duties and your responsibilities. Everything you do has some effect upon others, as do their actions upon you. And yet you must find out how to live your own life, use your own mind, go on toward the dream you wish to make real and solid. Know thyself said the ancient Greek philosophers, and this remains key advice for the man who would be in all ways wealthy. Without knowing yourself and being yourself, you cannot truly use the one Great Secret which gives you power to mold your future and make life carry you the way you want to go.

Let us then take off on our trip to Happy Valley!

Do not think of me as a back-seat driver. Rather, you are at the wheel and I merely call your attention to a trustworthy road map whereon the main highway is marked beyond question. On your journey to riches and peace of mind, the road grows smoother and straighter as you travel.

Never believe you don't have what it takes. Probably you are reading under an electric light. You know that Thomas A. Edison gave the first practical electric light to the world. But did you know that Edison was thrown out of school in the early grades after his teacher decided he had an "addled" mind and could not take schooling?

This then was the impact of another person's opinion upon Thomas Edison—to let him know with the voice of authority that he didn't have what it takes to absorb even a primary education! Where would he have been if he had allowed this directive to take charge of his thinking?

Fortunately for him and fortunately for the world, Edison decided to live his own life. Through early adversity, Edison discovered something he might never have learned through formal schooling. He learned, first, that he had a mind he could control and direct toward any desired end. Then he learned he could use the technical training of other men and successfully direct scientific research even though he himself never had been schooled in any of the sciences. When he took full possession of that "addled" mind it produced not only the incandescent lamp but also one great discovery after another.

A boy finds a friend and finds himself. I too was nearly doomed by a false label of unworthiness. I was then nine years old. My mother had died a year before, and I lived with relatives. To them and to my own father I was a problem child who never would accomplish anything save, perhaps, what a life of crime can accomplish.

I was doing my best to live up to my reputation as the successor of Jesse James. I even had a six-shooter which I had learned to handle like an expert. Then a certain woman came upon the scene and she changed my life. That woman was my stepmother.

Long before she arrived I had been thoroughly conditioned by my relatives to hate her. I found this very easy to do. She arrived, and my father brought her to our house where the relatives had gathered to meet her. He introduced her all around. At length he found me, where I stood in a corner doing my very best to look tough.

"And here," said my father, "is your stepson, Napoleon, beyond doubt the meanest boy in Wise County. We don't expect much good from him. I wouldn't be surprised if he starts throwing rocks at you by tomorrow morning."

At that moment, I believe my life hung in the balance.

It was a wise and wonderful woman who placed her hand under my stubborn chin and raised my head so that she could look me squarely in the eyes. She said only a few words, but they lifted me onto an entirely new level.

Turning to my father, my stepmother said: "You are wrong about this boy. He is not the meanest boy in Wise County or anywhere else. He is a very alert and intelligent boy, and all he needs is some worthy objective toward which to direct his very good mind."

That was the first time in my life that anyone had said anything good about me. I straightened up, threw out my chest and grinned. Then and there I sensed that "that woman" who had come to take my mother's place—as my relatives referred to her—was one of those rare people who can help others find the best that is in them.

That was the end of my six-shooter days. Increasingly finding myself as I grew older, I discovered my talent for writing. My stepmother helped me master the typewriter. With the aid of the typewriter I became a writer for newspapers.

Through that experience I qualified to interview successful men, and thus I came to sit down with Andrew Carnegie. Out of that interview—which ran on through the better part of three days and nights—came my commitment to search out the secret of successful achievement, not merely as a matter of words, but as a pattern of definite action in the lives of men who have achieved great wealth. Out of this grew the organization of the Science of Personal Achievement which has reverberated around the world, bringing prosperity and peace of mind to millions of men and women.

Great artists also live their own lives, or they could not be great. One of the great opera stars of all time, Madame Schumann-Heink, as a young girl went to a music teacher to have her voice tested. He listened a few minutes, then said brusquely: "That's enough! Go back to your sewing machine. You may become a first-class seamstress. A singer, no!"

Remember, that was the voice of authority speaking. The girl could have been forgiven for deciding then and there that she would never sing again. Yet she had and kept possession of her own mind. She became all the more determined that she would learn to sing and to sing well. This she did, and the world became richer. So it has been with many another case in which great personal talent might have been lost forever if the possessor of that talent had not felt it even when the "experts" said it was not there.

Adversity? It's a tonic, not a stumbling block! Every adversity carries the seed of an equal or greater benefit. Very few march straight to success without going through periods of temporary failure and discouragement. Yet when you are in possession of your inner self there is no such thing as a knockout blow. You may be knocked down, but you can bounce right back. You may detour on rough roads, but you always can find your way back to the paved highway.

You may think this applies only to simple matters. Think, then, of the infinitely complex matter of winning the independence of a colonial territory—and not only that, but of focusing the many scattered influences which make sure you become the country's first President.

SET REALISTIC GOALS

In 1910 I became the personal counselor of Manuel L. Quezon. I not only counseled him politically but, perhaps more importantly, I taught him the Science of Personal Achievement which then was quite new.

Señor Quezon was the first President of the Philippine Islands when they gained their freedom. In 1910, however, that time was far in the future. The goal of freeing his people possessed Quezon's mind, and he saw himself as the first President of the new nation. I assured him he could realize both ambitions, yet we knew that such great events do not come to pass overnight.

There is a well-recognized power in setting up a definite goal. Few, however, realize the power of setting a realistic time limit in which one intends to attain that goal. After having counseled Senor Quezon for some years, I induced him to set a definite time limit for freeing the Philippines and becoming the new nation's leader.

I also prepared an affirmation which he repeated to himself daily. It closed with a statement of this nature: "I will allow no person's opinion, no influence to enter my mind which does not harmonize with my purpose." Both the time limit and the affirmation were of great help to Quezon in knowing his own mind and keeping his own direction in the face of the enormous difficulties which beset him.

Twenty-four years and six months from the day Quezon began to use the Science of Personal Achievement, he became the first President of the free Philippine Islands.

Coincidence? Coincidence despite a world war which intervened and many other factors which were not foreseeable? I do not think it was a coincidence, for I have seen this principle of Personal Achievement work for so many people in so many different situations that coincidence must be ruled out.

We shall touch upon the principle again. Right now I shall tell you about just one man, presently doing business in Chicago, who has used it with notable success.

W. Clement Stone was in high school when he discovered his own goals, his own direction in which the powers of his own mind would take him. Soon he was selling insurance at such a rate that he made more money than his teachers. Today his fortune is estimated at more than $160 million and it is increasing rapidly.

In 1939, however, he faced disaster. At that time he was the head of an agency, representing a big casualty company, which sold a special accident and health policy. One day the parent company "pulled the string" and terminated his contract with two weeks' notice.

Mr. Stone did not have large reserves. It was imperative to keep that contract going. He spent forty-five minutes in refreshing his contact with his inner self; then he decided that within those critical two weeks he would persuade the casualty company it was against their own best interest to terminate his contract. The company had very cogent reasons for ending the contract. Nevertheless, they did change their minds as he wished them to and Stone kept on marching toward his fortune.

He then decided that by 1956 he would own his own big health and accident insurance company. By 1956 he did.

He decided that by 1956 he would have $10 million dollars of his own. He did.

I heard recently that Mr. Stone has set up a lifetime goal of $600 million. I do not know his deadline date, but I have no doubt that on or before that date he will have the stated sum; and further, that he will use a good part of it as he always has used his money—to benefit mankind. The concept of $600 million may frighten a man who thinks small, but a man who knows the secrets of Personal Achievement merely says: Why not?

A little while ago I made a survey for the purpose of learning who were the ten men who had made the most outstanding application of the Science of Personal Achievement in the United States.

W. Clement Stone was third from the top of the list. The other two were Andrew Carnegie, the sponsor of my twenty years of research, and Thomas Alva Edison, the greatest inventor of all time.

I met Mr. Stone for the first time in 1953. It was then that I began to unravel the dramatic story of his rise to fame and fortune, starting in business for himself with only one hundred dollars in cash and a copy of my most popular book, *Think and Grow Rich*. I was so intrigued by the effective application Stone had made of my success philosophy that I accepted his offer to help him take the Science of Personal Achievement to his entire insurance personnel.

The task covered ten years during which I devoted all of my time to helping Mr. Stone indoctrinate his entire organization with my success philosophy. It was a tremendous job but it paid off in terms which proved conclusively that my twenty years of research under the direction of Andrew Carnegie had uncovered a miraculous formula for helping people to get from where they were to where they wished to be in life.

When I first began my association with Mr. Stone, many of his top executives frowned upon the alliance as being a waste of time. They had never heard of a success philosophy based upon what five hundred outstanding men had learned from a lifetime of experience through the trial and error method, and they were naturally suspicious of it.

Five years later these same executives met with Mr. Stone and myself in a business conference. To my great surprise Mr. Stone arose and addressed himself to the group. "Gentlemen," said he, "the Combined Insurance Company of America is now performing miracles." Then a long pause, after which he said—"The company was performing no miracles before Napoleon Hill came here."

When I began my association with Mr. Stone the annual premium income from policy holders was around $24 million, and Mr. Stone's personal fortune was estimated to be around $3 million. When the association was discontinued by mutual consent ten years later, the annual premium income of the company was around $84 million and Mr. Stone's personal fortune was estimated to be more than $160 million.

How much did I get from the association? you may wish to ask. The cash I received was negligible in comparison with that which Mr. Stone received, but I was not working for monetary reward; I was after something far greater than that which could have been gained by any amount of money, for I had proved during those ten years of association with Mr. Stone that the Science of Personal Achievement could perform miracles for those who embraced it and made intelligent application of it.

More important still, I had laid the foundation for the Napoleon Hill Academy, which is now organizing and conducting franchise schools for the teaching of the Science of Personal Achievement throughout the United States and eventually will reach throughout the free world. The far-flung significance of these schools may be brought into understandable focus by the fact that the Science of Personal Achievement has turned out to be a perfect antidote for communism; something I had not anticipated when I began the organization of the philosophy in 1908. Which reminds me that, truly, "man proposes but God disposes."

THE SCIENCE BEHIND PERSONAL ACHIEVMENT

It may well be that the Science of Personal Achievement will become a strong factor in neutralizing the cancerous evil known as communism, which now threatens the liberty of all mankind.

The Science of Personal Achievement is already under option to a group of men who are having it translated into Spanish for the purpose of taking it to the people of all Spanish-speaking countries, starting with our Latin-American friends of the South. I plan eventually to have the philosophy translated into all the major languages of the world.

So, who is wise enough to say what I got from my ten years of association with W. Clement Stone, or wise enough to understand the hand of fate which brought the two of us together?

Arnold Reed is another insurance executive whose life story and its relation to the Science of Personal Achievement parallels that of W. Clement Stone. In many respects his story, as it related to the success philosophy, is more dramatic than the Stone story.

Mr. Reed was a top-ranking life insurance salesman, with a record of sales production seldom equaled by anyone in this field. Mr. Reed's sales started at around one million dollars annually and pyramided upward far beyond this amount. He was associated with an insurance company headed by a man whom he regarded as his personal friend.

Unfortunately (or was it?) Arnold had not read carefully the fine print of his contract with the company, for he learned later that it contained a clause which deprived him of his renewal premium commissions, the one factor in the insurance salesman's work which gives him his greatest incentive to do a good job.

This discovery shocked Arnold so severely that he went home and went to bed, refusing to eat or to communicate with his friends. Doctors were called in to diagnose his ailment but not one of them could find anything wrong with him physically. It was not his body that was sick, it was his soul, for the shock he had experienced through the perfidy of his friend had cut the line of communication between him and the source of inspiration which had made him a great life insurance salesman; that source which alone can make men truly great!

Slowly but surely Arnold Reed was dying.

His ailment was one that no doctor could cure. The doctors who had attended him knew this and frankly admitted they could offer no hope. Then a miracle happened. A friend of Arnold's, who had long been a student of my success philosophy, visited Arnold and presented him with *Think and Grow Rich*. "Here is a book," he told Arnold, "which has worked wonders for me and I want you to read it."

Arnold took the book, threw it on the bed beside him and turned away without comment. Hours later he picked up the book, opened it and, lo! something in it caught his eye and he read it through. Then he read it again, and again, and on the third time around he felt the surge of a power which he readily recognized as one which could bring him out of the dungeon of despair into which he had fallen.

He got out of bed and began to write letters to his friends who knew of his record as a life insurance salesman, offering them an opportunity to join with him in organizing a life insurance company under the name of Great Commonwealth Life Insurance Company.

The friends responded quickly and generously. The amount of money needed was oversubscribed and much of it had to be returned to the senders. All of this took place at about the time I was beginning my alliance with W. Clement Stone.

Now, some twelve years later, the Great Commonwealth Life Insurance Company is one of the most successful in its field, with a gross premium income of over $9 million in 1966, and rapidly increasing toward the new goal which Arnold Reed has set at a billion dollars annually.

The company is operating in a major portion of the United States and it has a sales organization of over four hundred dedicated men and women who have tuned in and drawn upon that mysterious power that brought Arnold Reed out of the shadows of death; and they are doing a job that is without parallel in the insurance industry.

The Great Commonwealth Life Insurance Company conducts schools in many parts of the country in which new recruits to its sales force are trained. The first thing each trainee receives is a copy of *Think and Grow Rich* and a briefing on what this book has done for Arnold Reed and the company.

The last time I spoke to the sales organization of the Great Commonwealth, Arnold Reed marched onto the platform holding me by the arm. He held up a copy of *Think and Grow Rich* as he said, "My friends, if it had not been for this book and my dear friend here on my left, there would have been no Great Commonwealth Life Insurance Company and I would now be six feet under the ground."

It was the shortest and the most dramatic introduction I had ever experienced, and it filled me so deeply with emotion that I could hardly begin my speech.

Arnold Reed is a truly great leader of men, as evidenced by the phenomenal record he has established with Great Commonwealth. The main secret of his leadership is his belief in what he is doing and his sincerity in his relationship with his associates, two qualities without which no man may become a great leader at any level of life.

A success-conscious mind functions rapidly and effectively. In my hundreds of interviews with men who had made fortunes, I noticed how well their minds were focused on success. Some of these men were well educated. Some, for example Henry Ford, were notably uninformed in some areas of "school learning." It never was the formal education or the lack of it which gave these men the power to use their minds with such drive and effect, nor was it unusual intelligence. What was it, then, which impelled their minds to seize upon great goals, then winnow all the circumstances of life and make use of what could help them achieve their ambitions? It was success consciousness.

First you must know your own mind; then you find success consciousness. When Henry Ford mastered the art of making a good, inexpensive automobile, he still went on using his success consciousness. He had to make sure his cars were well distributed and their sale pushed in every part of the country. For this he needed capital. The bankers had capital to lend, but he did not want outside financial interests to take hold of his company.

Ford's truly efficient mind showed him the way to get the capital he needed even while he built up his distributing organization. First, he allotted his entire output of automobiles only to distributors who held the Ford franchise. Then he made it clear that each distributor must accept a fixed quota of cars, advancing in cash a percentage of the purchase price before the cars were delivered.

This plan made every distributor practically a partner in the Ford business, yet it did not affect Mr. Ford's control of the business. Again, without affecting his control, it provided him with the necessary operating capital. Moreover, it provided his dealers with a very definite incentive toward finding a buyer for every car—actually the same incentive they would have had if they had been operating their own independent businesses.

I have heard it said that this plan worked a hardship on some of the Ford distributors. Having known some dealers since before the Model T car, however, and having looked at today's record, I can say that most Ford dealers are noteworthy for their success.

SUCCESS AND FAILURE—A CONSCIOUS CHOICE?

Two bicycle mechanics, Orville and Wilbur Wright, gave the world its first successful airplane. What kept their minds clicking, caused them first to build the world's first wind tunnel, caused them to find a secret of wingtip control which nobody else had thought of? What caused them to surmount limitations of material and of power which still make that first flight look "impossible"? First they took control of their own minds and their own lives; then they were guided by the success consciousness which always follows.

Is today's world different? Only in some details. Take such a device as a memory core, a tiny magnetic gadget which operates by the thousands in many modern computers. The Wright brothers did not know of such things, nor did Henry Ford or Andrew Carnegie or Thomas Edison. A young man named Merlyn Mickelson, in 1955, looked at the rapidly dawning computer age and saw what every age offers—a need and a way to fill it. He started to manufacture memory cores in his basement. His first investment in tools and supplies came to $7.21. His first employees were friends and neighboring housewives who "pitched in." Today, not yet forty, Mr. Mickelson still makes memory cores. He is President and 75 per cent owner of a $16-million-year company, and the company stock he holds is worth about $47 million.

Can success consciousness be instilled into a mind already filled with a record of failure? When you come to know your own mind and live your own life, you can wipe out a record of failure just as surely as you can erase the message on a tape recorder, leaving a wonderfully receptive tape—or mind—to receive new and better impressions.

Some people have been able to do this for themselves. Others need help. I well remember a man I helped to find himself. As you will see, I got him started and once he knew where he was going, he did the rest.

This was a dead-broke man just out of the Army. I believe he used the Army as a refuge, but eventually he was back in civilian clothes, looking for a job. The mere mention of "hard times" seemed to be enough to flatten him. He was shabby. He was hungry. He was willing to settle for crumbs if only he could get them.

He came to see me about finding work. At the outset he announced: "All I want is a place to sleep and enough to eat."

A place to sleep and enough to eat—in a world that throbs with riches!

Something prompted me to ask: "Why settle for a meal ticket? How would you like to become a millionaire?"

He looked at me with glassy eyes, swaying. "Please don't joke with me."

"I assure you I'm serious. Every man has some kind of assets, and every man can turn his assets into a million dollars or many millions if he uses them correctly."

He sighed. "What do you mean by assets? I have a nickel in my pocket."

"Bring your mind around to the positive side," I said, "and you have the most important asset you'll ever have. We'll work on that. Now let's take inventory of your skills. Sit down, we'll talk better. What did you do in the Army?"

He had been a cook. Before going into the Army he had been a Fuller Brush salesman. He was a good cook, I discovered, but obviously he had not been a good salesman. Still, he knew something about selling and in talking to him, I discovered he still wanted to sell. At the outset, however, he had no belief he ever could become a good salesman. The memory of past failures inhibited him and I had to help him break those self-inflicted mental blocks and see, not what he had been, but what he could be.

We talked for some time and meanwhile my own mind was busily at work. My mind was not weakened by hunger and hopelessness. There had been a time when my mind had known as much despair as did his; but now I was filled with success consciousness.

Questing about, my uninhibited mind remembered that special new kinds of cookware were now being developed. A new kind of cookware of great benefit to the housewife—a man who could think about cooking and even demonstrate—a man who could be made into a good salesman—and there we had the winning combination.

"Suppose you represented a company that makes a new kind of aluminum cookware," I said. "This cookware offers many advantages. It should be seen in action; then it will practically sell itself. Any housewife, for a small consideration—say, some free pots or pans for her own use—should be glad to invite her neighbors in for a home-cooked dinner. You cook that dinner with the special cookware, and after dinner you take orders for complete, matched sets. If twenty ladies are present, I'm sure you could induce half of them to purchase. Some of these would be eager to run similar dinner parties in their own homes. The business would become self-perpetuating."

"Sounds okay," my young soldier friend replied. "But where am I going to sleep meanwhile? And where am I going to eat? And where am I going to get a few clean shirts and a new suit? Not to mention the question of where I am going to get some money or credit to get started on?"

Such questions are typical of the mind which does not yet know itself, and so sums up all the obstacles rather than looking directly at the goal.

"Get yourself into the right frame of mind," I said, "and you will either find what you need or find a way to do without and still achieve your goal. When your mind can truly picture a desired goal, and feel success consciousness driving it toward that goal, you can win that goal. Let us put aside all other matters and investigate your state of mind."

Actually the young man was very close to having the desired positive state of mind. I waited till I was sure he had it, however. Then I said he was a good risk, and I gave him the use of our guest room, and his meals. I let him use my charge account at Marshall Field's so that he could be well dressed. I guaranteed his note for his first outfit of cookware.

During his first week he cleared nearly one hundred dollars in profit. The second week he doubled that amount. In a little while he began to train other men and women, whom he managed. Most of all, he instilled in them the success consciousness which now had full hold of his mind, and as they prospered, so did he.

At the end of four years, the young man who had been so hungry and broken-spirited, so very far from being a millionaire, was worth more than four million dollars. Moreover, his newly keen and efficient mind had perfected a home-demonstration selling plan which now nets millions of dollars annually to a large corps of salespeople.

LEARN HOW TO CONTROL YOUR MIND TO CONTROL YOUR LIFE

When a man finds his own mind and fills it with successful consciousness, or when another man helps him do so, I fancy that the bells of heaven ring with joy. Here is one more soul who has broken the chains forged by his fearful imagination.

Now you can see why I chose to begin this book by revealing what it means to take possession of your own mind, live your own life, find your real self that has no limitations. When you do this you have an asset worth whatever values you choose to make it worth.

Think again of what is involved in creating an independent nation. Think of ancient India with its teeming millions, under

British rule for generation after generation. Think of the Mahatma Gandhi, a man who had no money, controlled no army, did not own a house, did not even own a pair of pants. Yet he had an asset which was greater than all the might of the British Empire—the capacity to take possession of his own mind and direct it toward purposes of his own choosing. He chose to free India, and he lived to see the achievement of his purpose.

Thanks to the influence of Mahatma Gandhi, my Science of Personal Achievement now has many millions of followers in India. Whether your goal is money, the well-being of others, or a combination of these—as well it may be—know that there is nothing beyond the power of a mind that knows itself and believes in its own capabilities.

The spiritual defenses within the castle of your mind. I have purposely used the word "defenses" in order to call your attention to its varying meanings. A mind that is "on the defensive" is not an open mind. It is more likely to be a frightened mind, full of excuses and evasions, and hardly capable of lifting its possessor's eyes to the far horizons of accomplishment. In speaking of spiritual defenses, then, I speak of nothing that is negative: rather I speak of certain areas within which one may withdraw and thus become more completely one's self.

Every successful person I have known has surrounded himself with these spiritual defenses in one way or another. I adopted the system, and have found it invaluable. Here is how it works.

Consider your mind to be laid out in the pattern of some medieval castles. At the center there is a tower, or "keep," which is impregnable as it can be made. Going outward from the keep you would come to a wall not so formidable; and again going outward you would come to another wall which serves as the first line of defense.

A person approaching the castle first would have to pass the outer wall. This wall of spiritual defense in your mind need not be very high. Anyone who has a legitimate excuse for entering your mind with his ideas can climb this wall. If he does not have a legitimate excuse, however, the wall discourages him. When you set up such a wall, others come to know it is there and you give yourself a valuable protection.

A person who passes the first line of defense now confronts the second line which you may set up on certain occasions and not on others. When your mind sets up this wall, nobody may climb it unless that person has something strongly in common with you, or something importantly beneficial to share with you at that moment.

The inmost castle of protection is the most important of all. It is small, barely big enough to surround you, but when your mind retreats within that keep it is removed from every outside influence. With me, only the Creator can penetrate my inmost spiritual castle. Find yours and you find a source of great strength. Here is where you can find your inmost thoughts, undisturbed by outside influences; and until you find this castle you never can know them. Here is where you can search all the values of a problem and find a solution which otherwise you might not see. Here, especially, is where your fully possessed mind reveals what can be done—and when you come out of your retreat you know that it will be done and that you will do it.

At first you may find it necessary to retreat physically from the world into a quiet room or perhaps to some place distant from your business and from people who know you. This often is a good idea even when you have practice in finding the most inmost privacy of your mind, because there are many physical circumstances which break into thought.

When you have several times retreated to your thick-walled keep, however, you will find you can enter it for a few seconds even in the midst of others who are talking all around you. I have seen many successful men do this, and thus illustrate some of the power to which they owe their success. It is a great renewer of the spirit, a kind of recharge of ability and self-confidence and abiding faith.

All that I have to say in this book is keyed to one Supreme Secret.

This Secret has been strongly sketched in throughout this chapter. You have seen it, and already it is beginning to penetrate your subconscious mind—which never forgets.

POINTS TO REMEMBER

1. Acquainting with your inner self can help you get your wishes.
2. Use your mind and think your own thoughts. The creator provided a brain for a reason.
3. The principle of personal achievement.

9

CLEAR THE COBWEBS FROM YOUR THINKING

You are what you think. But what *do* you think? How orderly are your thought processes? How straight is your thinking?

And how clean are your thoughts?

There are certain mental cobwebs that clutter up the thinking of almost everyone, even the most brilliant minds. *Negative:* feelings, emotions, passions—habits, beliefs, and prejudices. Our thoughts become entangled in these webs.

Sometimes we have undesirable habits and we want to correct them. And there are times when we are strongly tempted to do wrong. Then, like an insect caught in a spider's web, we struggle to get free. Our conscious *will* is in conflict with our imagination and the *will* of our subconscious mind. The more we struggle, the more we become entrapped.

Some persons give up and experience the mental conflicts of a living hell. Others learn how to tap and use the powers of the subconscious through the conscious mind. They are victorious. And success through a positive mental attitude teaches you how to tap and use these powers.

An insect may not be able to avoid being caught in the spider's web. And when once trapped, it is unable to free itself. There is one thing, however, over which each person has absolute, inherent control, and that is his mental attitude. We can avoid mental cobwebs. We can clear them. And we can sweep them away as they begin to develop. We can free ourselves when once enmeshed. And we can *remain* free.

You do this by accurate thinking with PMA. Accurate thinking is one of the 17 success principles revealed in *Success Through a Positive Mental Attitude.*

To think accurately you must use reason. The science of reasoning or accurate thinking is called *logic.* One can learn it from books written specifically on this subject, such as: *The Art of Clear Thinking,* by Rudolf Flesch; *Your Most Enchanted Listener,* by Wendell Johnson; *Introduction to Logic,* by Irving Copi; and *The Art of Straight Thinking,* by Edwin Leavitt Clarke. These books can be of immense practical help.

But we don't act from reason alone. And action based on common sense is the result of more than just reason. It depends upon habits of thought and action, intuitions, experiences, and other influences such as tendencies and environment.

One of the cobwebs of our thinking is to assume that we act from reason alone when in reality every conscious act is the result of doing what we want to do. We make decisions. There is a tendency, when reasoning, to draw conclusions favorable to the strong *inner urges* of our subconscious mind. And this tendency exists in everyone—even the great thinkers and philosophers.

In 31 B.C. a Greek philosopher who lived in a city on the Aegean Sea wanted to go to Carthage. He was a teacher of logic; therefore he contemplated reasons in favor of making the voyage and reasons against it. For every reason as to why he should go he found that there were many more reasons why he shouldn't. Of course he would be seasick. The boat was so small that a storm might jeopardize his life. Pirates with swift sailing vessels were lying in wait off Tripoli to prey upon merchant vessels. If his ship were captured by them, they would take his worldly goods and sell him into slavery. Discretion indicated that he should *not* make the trip.

But he did. Why? *Because he wanted to.*

It so happens that emotion and reason should be in balance in everyone's life. Neither should always hold the controlling hand. So *sometimes* it is good to do what you want to do instead of what reason *fears*. As to this philosopher—he had a most pleasant journey and arrived back home safely.

Then there was Socrates, the great Athenian philosopher who lived from 470 B.C. to 399 B.C. He has gone down in history as one of the outstanding thinkers of all time. Wise as Socrates was, there were cobwebs in his thinking, too.

As a young man Socrates fell in love with Xanthippe. She was very beautiful. He wasn't good looking, but he was persuasive. Persuasive individuals seem to have the ability to get what they want. Socrates was successful in persuading Xanthippe to marry him.

Are you seeing only the mote in the other fellow's eye? After the honeymoon was over, things didn't go along so well at his house. His wife began to see his faults. And he saw hers. He was motivated by egoism. He was selfish. She was always nagging him. Socrates reportedly said, "My aim in life is to get on well with people. I chose Xanthippe because I knew if I could get on well with her, I could get along with anyone."

That is what he said. But his actions disproved his words. It is questionable that he tried to get on well with more than a few. When you always try to prove to persons whom you meet that they are wrong, you repel rather than attract as Socrates did.

Yet he said that he endured Xanthippe's nagging for his own personal self-discipline. But he would have developed real self-discipline had he tried to understand his wife and to influence her through the same considerate attentions and expressions of love that he used in persuading her to marry him. He didn't see the beam in his own eye, but he saw the mote in Xanthippe's eye.

Of course, Xanthippe wasn't blameless either. Socrates and she were just like many husbands and wives living today. After their marriage they neglect to continue to communicate their true feelings of affection, understanding, and love to each other. They neglect to continue to employ the same pleasing personalities and mental attitudes that made their courtship such a happy experience. Negligence is a cobweb, too.

Now Socrates didn't read *Success Through a Positive Mental Attitude*. Neither did Xanthippe. Had she done so, she would have known how to motivate her husband so that their home life would have been a happier one. She would have seen the beam in her eye, rather than the mote in Socrates'. She would have controlled her own reactions and been sensitive to the reactions of her husband. In fact, she might have even proved the fallacy of his logic.

And because the story of Socrates proves he saw only the mote in Xanthippe's eye we shall tell you about another young man—he learned to see the beam in his own eye. But before we do, let's see how the habit of nagging develops.

INSTEAD OF QUESTIONING OTHERS, QUESTION YOURSELF

You see, when you know the cause of a problem, you can often avoid it. Or you can find your own solution to that problem if you already have it. S. I. Hayakawa in *Language in Thought and Action* wrote:

> In order to cure (what she believes to be) her husband's faults, a wife may nag him. His faults get worse, so she nags him some more. Naturally his faults get worse still, and she nags him even more. Governed by a fixated reaction to the problem of her husband's faults, she can meet it only one way. The longer she continues, the worse it gets, until they are both nervous wrecks; their marriage is destroyed, and their lives are shattered.

Now what about the young man? It was the first evening of a PMA Science of Success class when he was asked, "Why are you taking this course?"

"Because of my wife!" he responded. Many of the students laughed— but not the instructor. He knew from experience that there are many unhappy homes when husband or wife sees the other's faults but not his or her own.

He restored happiness to his home. It was four weeks later in a private conference that the instructor asked the student, "How are you coming along with your problem?"

"It's solved!"

"That's wonderful! But how did you solve it?"

"I learned: *when I am faced with a problem that involves misunderstandings with other persons, I must first start with myself.* When I examined my own mental attitude, I discovered that it was negative. My problem was really not with my wife after all—it was with me! In solving my problem I found that I no longer had one with her."

Now, what if Socrates had said to himself: "When I am faced with a problem that involves a misunderstanding with Xanthippe, I must first start with myself "? And what would happen if you would say to yourself: "When I am faced with a problem that involves a misunderstanding with another person, I must first start with myself "? Would your life be a happier one?

But there are many other cobwebs that interfere with happiness. Oddly enough, the one that is the greatest hindrance is the very tool of thought itself: *words.* Words are symbols, as S. I. Hayakawa tells us in his book. And you will find that a one-word symbol can mean to you the sum total of a combination of innumerable ideas, concepts, and experiences. And you will also see as you continue to read *Success Through a Positive Mental Attitude* that the subconscious instantaneously communicates to the conscious mind through symbols.

Through one word you can motivate others to act. When you say to another person "You can!" this is *suggestion*. When you say to yourself "I can!" you motivate yourself by *self-suggestion*. But more about these universal truths in the next chapter. First let's recognize that a whole science has grown up around the important discoveries made about words and the communicating of ideas through words: the science of semantics.

And Hayakawa is an expert in this field. He tells us that to find out what a word really means on the lips of another person, or even on your own lips, is essential in the process of accurate thinking.

But how does one do this?

Just be *specific*. Start with a meeting of the minds and many needless misunderstandings will be avoided.

One word can cause an argument. The uncle of a nine-year-old boy was visiting in the home of the boy's parents. One evening when the father came home, the following dialogue developed:

"What do you think of a boy that lies?"

"I don't think very much of him, and I know one thing certain: my son tells the truth."

"He told a lie today."

"Son, did you tell your uncle a lie?"

"No, Father."

"Let's clear this thing up. Your uncle says you lied. You say you didn't. Just exactly what did happen?" he asked, turning to the uncle.

"Well, I told him to take his toys down to the basement. He didn't do it, and he told me that he did."

"Son, did you take your toys to the basement?"

"Yes, Father."

"Son, how do you explain this? Your uncle says that you didn't take your toys to the basement and you say that you did."

"There are several steps leading from the first floor down to the basement... About four steps down is a window... I put my toys on the windowsill...The basement is the distance between the floor and the ceiling... My toys *are* in the basement!"

The argument between the uncle and his nephew was due to the definition of one word: basement. The boy probably knew what his uncle meant, but he was lazy and hadn't wanted to run all the way downstairs. When he was faced with punishment, the boy tried to save himself by using logic to prove his point.

Now this may be intriguing. But more motivating will be the story of a young man who didn't know what the most important word symbol in any language means. And what is the most important word in any language? That word is *God.*

Not so long ago a student from Columbia University called on the Rev. Harry Emerson Fosdick, Minister Emeritus of The Riverside Church of New York City. The student had hardly gotten through the door before he said: "I am an atheist!" When he sat down, he repeated defiantly, "I don't believe in God."

IMPORTANCE OF ASKING THE RIGHT QUESTIONS

Let's start with a meeting of the minds. Now, fortunately, Dr. Fosdick was also an expert in the field of semantics. He knew from long experience that he could never really communicate with another person unless he understood exactly what that other person meant by the words he used. He also knew that it was necessary for the other person to comprehend his meaning. So instead of taking offense at the student's brash remark, Dr. Fosdick expressed a genuinely friendly interest in him and then asked, "Please describe to me the God you do not believe in."

The young man had to think, as everyone has to think when he is asked a question that doesn't cause a reflex "yes" or "no" answer. Dr. Fosdick knew that the right question could sweep strong cobwebs of negative thinking out of the youth's mind.

After a little while the student began to try to describe the God he didn't believe in. In so doing he gave the minister a very clear picture of the God he rejected.

"Well," said Dr. Fosdick when the student had finished, "if that is the God you don't believe in, I don't believe in him either. So we are both atheists. Nevertheless," he continued, "we still have the universe on our hands. What do you make of it—its formation, its meaning?"

Before the young man left Dr. Fosdick, he discovered that he was not an atheist at all, but a very good theist. He did believe in God.

Now Dr. Fosdick had not been thrown by the undefined use of a word. In this instance he helped sweep away the cobwebs of the young man's thinking by asking him questions. The simple, clear response as to what the young man didn't believe in was enough to allow a meeting of the minds. The second question directed the youth's thoughts into the proper channels. And it gave Dr. Fosdick an opportunity to explain his meaning of the universal God.

Frog legs taught him logic. As we have seen, the student reached two entirely different conclusions. Each was based on a different premise. Cobwebs will interfere with accurate thinking and cause you to reach a wrong conclusion when you start with a false premise. W. Clement Stone had an amusing experience with this which he describes as follows:

As a boy I enjoyed eating frog legs. One day at a restaurant I was served jumbo frog legs and didn't like them. Then and there I decided that I didn't like large frog legs.

Some years later I was at a quality restaurant in Louisville, Kentucky and saw frog legs on the menu. My conversation with the waiter was as follows:

"Are these small frog legs?"

"Yes sir!"

"Are you sure? I don't like the large ones."

"Yes sir!"

"If they're the small ones, that'll be fine for me."

"Yes sir!"

When the waiter brought the entrée, I saw that they were jumbo frog legs. I was irritated and said: "These aren't the small frog legs!"

"These are the smallest we could find, sir," the waiter responded.

Rather than be unpleasant I ate the frog legs. And I enjoyed them so much that I wished they had been larger.

I learned a lesson in logic.

In analyzing the matter I realized that my conclusions about the merits of large and small frog legs had been based on the wrong premise. It wasn't the size of the frog legs that made them distasteful. It was the fact that the jumbo frog legs I had eaten the first time hadn't been fresh. I had associated my distaste for jumbo frog legs with size rather than with spoilage.

Now we see that cobwebs prevent accurate thinking when we start with the wrong premise. So many persons think inaccurately when they allow all-embracing word symbols to clutter up their minds with false premises. Such words or expressions as: always—only—never—nothing—every—everyone—no one—can't—impossible—either—or—are most frequently false premises. Consequently, when they are so used their logical conclusions are false.

Necessity plus PMA can motivate you to succeed. Now there is one word which, when used with PMA, motivates a person to honorable achievement. When used with NMA, it becomes the excuse for lies, deception, and fraud. *Necessity* is the word. Necessity is the mother of invention and the father of crime.

Inviolable standards of integrity are fundamental to all worthwhile achievement and are an integral part of PMA.

You will read many success stories throughout this book in which persons are motivated by *necessity*. And in each case you'll find that such persons achieved success without transgressing an inviolable standard of integrity. Lee Braxton is such a man.

THE NECESSITY OF FINDING A GOAL

Lee Braxton, of Whiteville, North Carolina, was the son of a struggling blacksmith. He was the tenth child in a family of twelve. "...So you might say," says Mr. Braxton, "that I became acquainted with poverty early in life. By hard work I managed to get through the sixth grade in school. I shined shoes, delivered groceries, sold newspapers, worked in a hosiery mill, washed automobiles, and served as a mechanic's helper."

When he became a mechanic, it appeared to Lee that he had risen as far as he could go. Perhaps he had not yet developed inspirational dissatisfaction. In due course he married. And together he and his wife scrimped along. He was used to poverty. And it now seemed to him that it was impossible for him to break the ties which held him down, although he was poorly paid and just barely supporting his family. The Braxtons were already having a terrible time making ends meet when, to complete the picture of defeat, he lost his job. His home was about to be taken from him because he was unable to meet the mortgage payments. It seemed a hopeless situation.

But Lee was a man of character. He was also a religious man. And he believed that *God is always a good God.* So he prayed for guidance. As if in answer to his prayer, he received the book *Think and Grow Rich* from a friend. This friend had lost his job and his home in the Depression. And he had been motivated to recoup his fortune after reading *Think and Grow Rich.*

Now Lee was ready.

He read the book again and again. He was searching for

financial success. He said to himself: "It seems to me there is something I have to do. I have to add something. No book will do it for me. The first thing I must do is develop a Positive Mental Attitude regarding my abilities and my opportunities. I must certainly choose a definite goal. When I do, I must aim higher than I have in the past. But I must get started. I'll begin with the first job I can find."

And he looked for a job and found one. It didn't pay much to start.

But it wasn't many years after he had read *Think and Grow Rich* that Lee Braxton organized and became president of the First National Bank of Whiteville, was elected mayor of his city, and engaged in many successful business enterprises. You see: Lee had aimed high—in fact, very high. He had taken as his major purpose the goal of being rich enough to retire at the age of 50. He achieved this goal six years ahead of time—retiring from active business with substantial wealth and a fine independent income at the age of 44. Today Lee Braxton is leading a useful life. He is devoting his entire efforts to helping Oral Roberts, the evangelist, in his ministry.

Now, the jobs that he took and the investments he made in climbing from failure to success are not important here. What is important is that *necessity motivates a man with PMA to action without transgressing recognized inviolable standards.* An honest man won't deceive, cheat, or steal because of necessity. *Honesty is inherent in PMA.*

Necessity, NMA, and crime. Now, contrast such a man with the many thousands of persons with NMA who are imprisoned because of stealing, embezzling, or other crimes. When you ask them why they stole in the first place, their answer invariably is: "I had to." And that's how they landed in prison! They allowed themselves to become dishonest because cobwebs in their thinking caused them to believe that necessity forces one to become dishonest.

Some years ago, while doing personal counseling in the prison library in the federal penitentiary at Atlanta, I had several confidential talks with Al Capone. In one of these talks, I inquired: "How did you get started in a life of crime?"

Capone answered with one word: "Necessity."

Then tears came into his eyes and he choked up. He began to tell of some of the good things he had done which the newspapers had never mentioned. Of course, these seem insignificant compared to the evil that is attributed to his name.

That unfortunate man wasted his life, destroyed his peace of mind, undermined his physical body with deadly disease, and spread fear and disaster in the path he followed—all because he never learned to clear the cobwebs of his thinking regarding *necessity.*

And when Capone told of his good deeds, which he implied offset to some great degree the wrongs he had done, he clearly indicated another cobweb which was preventing him from thinking accurately. While a man can neutralize the evil he has done by true repentance followed by a life of good deeds, Capone was not such a man.

But there was such a man. He was a teenage problem child. Yet his mother never lost hope even though many of her specific prayers for him seemed unanswered. And she never lost faith, regardless of her son's escapades or wrongdoing.

He was a teenage problem child. This young man became an educated, intellectual, passionate, and sensual teenage problem child. He took pride in being first, even in evil. It is said that he disobeyed his parents and teachers, lied and deceived, committed petty thefts, cheated in gambling, indulged in alcoholic and sexual excesses.

Yet because of his mother's constant and earnest pleas to him to mend his ways, *he struggled to find himself* even before he reached the lowest point in his moral life. Sometimes he was filled with shame by the knowledge that men with less education were able to resist temptations which he thought he was powerless to resist. And because he was educated, and because he was searching, he studied the Bible and other inspirational books of his day.

Even so, he lost many battles with himself. And then one day he won the battle that turned the tide to personal victory. This is what happens when a person *keeps trying*. It was during a period of remorse when he was overcome with self-condemnation that he overheard a conversation in which one voice said, *"Take up and read!"*

He reached for the nearest book, opened it, and read: "Let us walk honestly, as in the day; not in rioting and drunkenness, not in chambering and wantonness, not in strife and envying. But put ye on the Lord Jesus Christ, and make not provision for the flesh, to fulfill the lusts thereof."

It often happens. After a person suffers a serious defeat in a personal battle with himself, he may at that point be ready. His remorse can be so emotional and sincere that he is motivated to take immediate action and through perseverance make the change that keeps him on the road to a complete victory.

Now this young man was ready!

POINTS TO REMEMBER

1. You are what you think.
2. Learn how to tap and use the powers of the subconscious through the conscious mind.
3. Words are the greatest hindrance towards happiness.

10

MOTIVATE YOURSELF AND OTHERS

Motivate yourself and others with the magic ingredient. What is the magic ingredient?

One man, in particular, found it. Here is his story.

Some years ago, this man, a successful cosmetic manufacturer, retired at the age of sixty-five.

Each year thereafter his friends gave him a birthday party, and on each occasion they asked him to disclose his formula. Year after year he pleasantly refused; however, on his seventy-fifth birthday his friends, half jokingly and half seriously, once again asked if he would disclose the secret.

"You have been so wonderful to me over the years that I now will tell you," he said. "You see, in addition to the formulas used by other cosmeticians, I added the magic ingredient."

"What is the magic ingredient?" he was asked.

"I never promised a woman that my cosmetics would make her beautiful, but I always gave her hope."

Hope is the magic ingredient! Hope is a desire with the expectation of obtaining what is desired and belief that it is obtainable. A person consciously reacts to that which to him is desirable, believable, and attainable.

And he also subconsciously reacts to the inner urge that induces action when environmental suggestion, self-suggestion, or autosuggestion cause the release of the powers of his subconscious mind. His response to suggestion may develop obedience that is direct, neutral, or in reverse action to a specific symbol. In other words, there may be various types and degrees of motivating factors.

Every result has a given cause. Your every act is the result of a given cause—your motives.

POINTS TO REMEMBER

1. Constantly motivate yourself and others.
2. Hope to attain what you desire acts as the best motivator.
3. Strengthen your will to fight your inner urges.

11

THE SUBCONSCIOUS MIND

THE SUBCONSCIOUS MIND consists of a field of consciousness in which every impulse of thought or sensation that reaches the objective mind through any of the five senses is classified and recorded, and from which thoughts may be recalled or withdrawn as letters may be taken from a filing cabinet.

The subconscious mind receives and files sense impressions or thoughts regardless of their nature. You may VOLUNTARILY plant in your subconscious mind any plan, thought, or purpose which you desire to translate into its physical or monetary equivalent. The subconscious acts first on the dominating desires which have been mixed with emotional feeling, such as FAITH.

THE SUBCONSCIOUS MIND WORKS DAY AND NIGHT.

Through a method or procedure that is not yet understood, the subconscious mind draws upon the forces of Infinite Intelligence for the power with which it voluntarily transmutes one's desires into their physical equivalent, making use always of the most practical media by which this end may be accomplished.

You cannot *entirely* control your subconscious mind, but you can voluntarily hand over to it any plan, desire, or purpose which you wish transformed into concrete form. There is plenty of evidence to support the belief that the subconscious mind is the connecting link between the finite human mind and Infinite

Intelligence. It is the intermediary through which one may draw upon the forces of Infinite Intelligence at will. It alone contains the secret process by which mental impulses are modified and changed into their spiritual equivalent. It alone is the medium through which prayer may be transmitted to the source which is capable of answering prayer.

The possibilities of creative effort connected with the subconscious mind are stupendous and imponderable. They inspire one with awe. I never approach the discussion of the subconscious mind without a feeling of littleness and inferiority, which is due, perhaps, to the fact that our entire stock of knowledge on this subject is so pitifully limited. The very fact that the subconscious mind is the medium of communication between the thinking human mind and Infinite Intelligence is in itself a thought which almost paralyzes one's reason.

After you have accepted as a reality the existence of the subconscious mind and *understand* its possibilities as a medium for transmuting your DESIRES into their physical or monetary equivalent, you will understand why you have been repeatedly admonished to MAKE YOUR DESIRES CLEAR AND TO REDUCE THEM TO WRITING. You will also understand the necessity of PERSISTENCE in carrying out instructions.

FORCE OF MANIFESTATION

The subconscious mind will not remain idle! If you fail to plant DESIRES in your subconscious mind, it will feed upon the thoughts which reach it as the *result of your neglect*.

For the present, it is sufficient if you remember that you are living *daily* in the midst of all manner of thought impulses which are reaching your subconscious mind without your knowledge or awareness. Some of these impulses are negative, some are positive. You are now engaged in trying to help shut off the flow of negative impulses and to aid in voluntarily influencing your subconscious mind through positive impulses of DESIRE.

When you achieve this, you will possess the key which unlocks the door to your subconscious mind. Moreover, you will control that door so completely that no undesirable thought will influence your subconscious mind.

Everything which human beings create BEGINS in the form of athought impulse. No one can create anything which he or she does not first conceive in THOUGHT. Through the aid of the imagination, thought impulses may be assembled into plans. The imagination, when under control, may be used for the creation of plans or purposes that lead to success in one's chosen occupation.

All thought impulses which are intended for transmutation into their physical equivalent and which are voluntarily planted in the subconscious mind must pass through the imagination and be mixed with faith. The mixing of faith with a plan, or purpose, intended for submission to the subconscious mind may be done ONLY through the imagination.

From these statements you will readily observe that the voluntary use of the subconscious mind calls for the coordination and application of all the principles of success explained in this book.

Ella Wheeler Wilcox gave evidence of her understanding of the powerof the subconscious mind when she wrote:

You never can tell what a thought will do
In bringing you hate or love—
For thoughts are things, and their airy wings
Are swifter than carrier doves.
They follow the law of the universe—
Each thing creates its kind,
And they speed o'er the track to bring you back
Whatever went out from your mind.

Mrs. Wilcox understood the truth that thoughts which go out from one's mind also embed themselves deeply in one's subconscious mind, where they serve as a magnet, pattern, or blueprint by which the subconscious mind is influenced while translating them into their physical equivalent. Thoughts are truly things, for the reason that every material thing begins in the form of "thought-energy."

The subconscious mind is more susceptible to influence by impulses of thought which are mixed with feeling or emotion than by those originating solely in the reasoning portion of the mind. In fact, there is much evidence to support the theory that ONLY emotionalized thoughts have any ACTION influence upon the subconscious mind. It is a well-known fact that emotion or feeling rules the majority of people. If it is true that the subconscious mind responds more quickly to, and is influenced more readily by, thought impulses which are energized with emotion, then it is essential to become familiar with the more important of the emotions. There are seven major positive emotions and seven major negative emotions. The negatives automatically inject themselves into the thought impulses, which ensures their passage into the subconscious mind. The positives *must be injected*, through the principle of autosuggestion, into the thought impulses which an individual wishes to pass on to his or her subconscious mind.

These emotions, or feeling impulses, may be likened to yeast in a loaf of bread because they constitute the ACTION element which transforms thought impulses from the passive to the active state. Thus may one understand why thought impulses which have been well mixed with emotion are acted upon more readily than thought impulses originating in cold reason.

You are preparing yourself to influence and control the "inner audience" of your subconscious mind in order to hand over to it the DESIRE for money, which you wish transmuted into its monetary equivalent. It is essential, therefore, that you understand the method of approach to this inner audience. You must speak its language or it will not heed your call. It understands best the language of emotion or feeling. Let me, therefore, describe here the seven major positive emotions and the seven major negative emotions, so that you may draw upon the positives and avoid the negatives when giving instructions to your subconscious mind.

THE SEVEN MAJOR POSITIVE EMOTIONS

The emotion of DESIRE
The emotion of FAITH
The emotion of LOVE
The emotion of SEX
The emotion of ENTHUSIASM
The emotion of ROMANCE
The emotion of HOPE

There are other positive emotions, but these are the seven most powerful and the ones most commonly used in creative effort. Master these seven emotions (they can be mastered only by USE), and the other positive emotions will be at your command when you need them. Remember, in this connection, that you are studying a book which is intended to help you develop money-consciousness by *filling your mind with positive emotions*. One does not become money-conscious by filling one's mind with negative emotions.

THE SEVEN MAJOR NEGATIVE EMOTIONS
(TO BE AVOIDED)

The emotion of FEAR
The emotion of JEALOUSY
The emotion of HATRED
The emotion of REVENGE
The emotion of GREED

The emotion of SUPERSTITION
The emotion of ANGER

Positive and negative emotions cannot occupy the mind at the same time. One or the other must dominate. It is your responsibility to make sure that positive emotions constitute the dominating influence of your mind. Here the LAW OF HABIT will come to your aid. *Form the habit* of applying and using the positive emotions! Eventually, they will dominate your mind so completely that the negatives *cannot* enter it.

Only by following these instructions literally, and continuously, can you gain control over your subconscious mind. The presence of a single powerful negative thought or feeling in your conscious mind is sufficient to *destroy* all chances of constructive aid from your subconscious mind.

PRAYER'S CODE OF CONDUCT

If you are an observant person, you must have noticed that most people resort to prayer ONLY AFTER everything else has FAILED! Or else they pray by a ritual of meaningless words. And because it is a fact that most people who pray do so ONLY AFTER EVERYTHING ELSE HAS FAILED, they go to prayer with their minds filled with FEAR and DOUBT, *which are the emotions the subconscious mind acts* upon and passes on to Infinite Intelligence. Likewise, those are the emotions which Infinite Intelligence receives and ACTS UPON.

If you pray for a thing, but have fear as you pray that you may not receive it or that your prayer will not be acted upon by Infinite Intelligence, your prayer *will have been in vain.*

Prayer does sometimes result in the realization of that for which one prays. If you have ever had the experience of receiving that for which you prayed, go back in your memory and recall your actual STATE OF MIND while you were praying, and you will know for sure that the theory here described is more than a theory.

The time may come when the schools and educational institutions of the country will teach the "science of prayer." When that time comes (it will come as soon as humanity is ready for it and demands it), no one will approach the Universal Mind (Infinite Intelligence) in a state of fear, for the very good reason that there will be no such emotion as fear. Ignorance, superstition, and false teaching will have disappeared, and human beings will have attained their true status as children of Infinite Intelligence. A few have already attained this blessing.

If you believe this prophesy is farfetched, take a look at the human race in retrospect. Less than a hundred years ago, people believed that lightning was evidence of the wrath of God and feared it. Now, thanks to the power of FAITH, we have harnessed lightning and made it turn the wheels of industry. Much less than a hundred years ago, people believed the space between the planets to be nothing but a great void, a stretch of dead nothingness. Now, thanks to this same power of FAITH, we know that far from being either dead or a void, the space between the planets is very much alive, that it is filled with mysterious substances and pulsates with energy—the highest form of energy known, except perhaps for the energy of THOUGHT! Moreover, there is evidence that this living, pulsating, vibratory energy which permeates every atom of matter and fills every niche of space, connects every human brain with other human brains in mysterious ways we do not yet understand.

Why should we not believe that this same energy connects every human brain with Infinite Intelligence? There are no tollgates between the finite human mind and Infinite Intelligence. The communication costs nothing except Patience, Faith, Persistence, Understanding, and a SINCERE DESIRE to communicate.

Moreover, the approach can be made only by each individual. Paid prayers are worthless. Infinite Intelligence does no business by proxy. You either go direct or you do not communicate. You may buy prayer books and repeat them until the day of your doom without avail. Thoughts which you wish to communicate to Infinite Intelligence must undergo transformation such as can be given only through your own subconscious mind. The method by which you may communicate with Infinite Intelligence is analogous to that through which the vibration of sound is communicated by radio. If you understand the working principle of radio, you know that sound cannot be communicated through the airwaves until it has been stepped up or changed into a rate of vibration which the human ear cannot detect. The radio processing and transmitting equipment takes the sound of the human voice and scrambles or modifies it by stepping up the vibration millions of times. Only in this way can the vibration of sound be communicated hundreds or thousands of miles away. After this transformation has taken place, the original vibrations of sound—now in the form of highly energized electromagnetic waves—are broadcast across the airwaves to radio receivers, which step that energy back down to its original state so that it is recognized as sound.

Similarly, the subconscious mind is the intermediary which translates one's prayers into terms which Infinite Intelligence utilizes, presents the message, and receives back the answer in the form of a definite plan or idea for procuring the object of the prayer. Understand this principle and you will know why mere words read from a prayer book—while they may provide comfort and give one cause for reflection and meditation—cannot and will never serve as an agency of active communication between the human mind and Infinite Intelligence. Before your prayer will "reach" Infinite Intelligence (a statement of this author's theory only), it is transformed in some way from its original "thought vibration" into terms of "spiritual vibration."

Faith is the only known agency which will give your thoughts a spiritual nature in this way. FAITH and FEAR make poor bedfellows. Where one is found, the other cannot exist.

POINTS TO REMEMBER

1. Don't underestimate the power of your subconscious mind.
2. The subconscious mind transmutes your desires into their physical equivalent.
3. Learn how to direct the thought-energy.

12

YOU CAN CHANGE YOUR MIND

If you are unhappy with your world and want to change it, the place to start is with yourself. *If you are right, your world will be right.* This is what PMA is all about. When you have a Positive Mental Attitude, the problems of your world tend to bow before you.

You were born a champion. Have you ever thought about the battles you won before you were born? "Stop and think about yourself," says Amram Scheinfeld, an expert on genetics. "In all the history of the world there was never anyone else exactly like you, and in all the infinity of time to come, there will never be another."

You are a very special person. And many struggles took place that had to be successfully concluded in order to produce you. Just think: tens of millions of sperm cells participated in a great battle, yet only one of them won—the one that made you! It was a great race to reach a single object: a precious egg containing a tiny nucleus. This goal for which the sperms were competing was smaller in size than the point of a needle. And each sperm was so small that it would have to be magnified thousands of times before it could be seen by the human eye. Yet it is on this microscopic level that your life's most decisive battle was fought.

The head of each of the millions of sperms contained a precious cargo of 24 chromosomes, just as there were 24 in the tiny nucleus of the egg. Each chromosome was composed of jelly-like beads closely strung together. Each bead contained hundreds of genes to which scientists attribute all the factors of your heredity.

The chromosomes in the sperm comprised all the hereditary material and tendencies contributed by your father and his ancestors; those in the egg-nucleus the inheritable traits of your mother and her ancestors. Your mother and father themselves represented the culmination of over two billion years of victory in the battle to survive. And then one particular sperm—the fastest, the healthiest, the winner—united with the waiting egg to form one, tiny living cell.

The life of the most important living person had begun. You had become a champion over the most staggering odds you will ever have to face. For all practical purposes you had inherited from the vast reservoir of the past all the potential abilities and powers you need to achieve your objectives.

You were born to be a champion, and no matter what obstacles and difficulties lie in your way, they are not one-tenth so great as the ones that have already been overcome at the moment of your conception. Victory is *built in* to every living person. Take the case of Irving Ben Cooper, who was one of America's most respected judges. But this was very far from the way young Ben Cooper thought of himself as a young boy.

How a frightened boy developed PMA. Ben grew up in a near-slum neighborhood in St. Joseph, Missouri. His father was an immigrant tailor who earned little money. Many days there simply wasn't enough to eat. To heat their small home, Ben used to take a coal scuttle, and walk down to the railroad tracks that ran nearby. There he would pick up pieces of coal. It embarrassed Ben to have to do it. He'd often try to sneak through the back streets so children from school wouldn't see him.

But they often did. There was one gang of boys in particular who found great sport in ambushing Ben on his way home from the tracks and beating him up. They would scatter his coal all over the street and send him home with tears streaming from his eyes.

Thus it was that Ben lived in a more or less permanent state of fear and self-despising.

Something happened, as it always must when we break the pattern of defeat. The victory within us does not assert itself until we are ready. Ben was inspired to positive action because he read a book. It was *Robert Coverdale's Struggle* by Horatio Alger.

In it Ben read the adventures of a youngster like himself who was faced with great odds, but who overcame these odds with the courage and moral strength which Ben wished to possess.

The boy read every one of the Horatio Alger books he could borrow. As he read, he lived the part of the hero. All winter he sat in the cold kitchen reading stories of courage and success, unconsciously absorbing a Positive Mental Attitude.

Some months after he had read his first Horatio Alger book, Ben Cooper was again making a trip down to the railroad tracks. Off in the distance he saw three figures dart behind a building. His first thought was to turn and run. Then he remembered the courage that he had admired in his book heroes, and, instead of turning, his hand gripped the coal scuffle more tightly and he marched straight ahead, *as if he were one of the Alger heroes.*

It was a brutal fight. The three boys jumped Ben all at the same time. His bucket dropped, and he started flailing his arms with a determination that caught the bullies by surprise. Ben's right hand smashed into the lips and nose of one of the boys—his left hand into his stomach. To Ben's surprise, the boy stopped fighting and turned and ran. Meanwhile the other two boys were hitting and kicking him. Ben managed to push one boy away and knock the other down. He jumped on the second boy with his knees, while he plowed punch after punch into his stomach and jaw—as if he were mad. Now there was just one boy left. This was the leader. He had jumped on top of Ben. Ben managed to pull him aside and get on his feet. For a second the two boys stood and looked each other squarely in the eyes.

And then, bit by bit, the leader stepped backwards. He, too, ran away. Perhaps it was righteous indignation, but Ben picked up a chunk of coal and threw it at the retreater.

It wasn't until then that Ben realized that his nose was bleeding and that he had black and blue marks on his body from the punches and kicks he had received. It was worth it! It was a great day in Ben's life. In that moment he overcame fear.

Ben Cooper wasn't much stronger than he had been a year earlier. His attackers were no less tough. The difference came in Ben's own mental attitude. He had faced danger in spite of fear. He decided that no longer was he going to be pushed around by bullies. From now on, he himself was going to change his world. And, of course, this is exactly what he did.

PRINCIPLES OF SUCCESS

Identify yourself with a successful image. The boy gave himself an identity. When he fought the three bullies on the street that day, he was not fighting as frightened, undernourished Ben Cooper. He was fighting as Robert Coverdale or any other of the plucky and daring heroes of Horatio Alger's books.

Identifying one's self with a successful image can help break the habits of self-doubt and defeat which years of NMA set up within a personality. Another and equally important successful technique for changing your world is to identify yourself with an image that will inspire you to make the right decisions. It can be a slogan, a picture, or any other symbol that is meaningful to you.

What will your picture say to you? The president of a midwest concern operating internationally was visiting his San Francisco office. He noticed a large photograph of himself on the wall of the office of Dorothy Jones, a private secretary. "Dotti, that's a rather large picture for this size room, isn't it?" he asked.

Dorothy responded, "When I have a problem, do you know

what I do?" Without waiting for an answer, she demonstrated by placing her elbows on her desk, propping her head on the fingers of her folded hands, and looking up at the picture. "Boss, how the heck would you solve this problem?" she asked.

Dotti's remarks seem rather humorous. Yet the essence of her idea is startling. Perhaps you have a picture in your office, your home, or in your wallet, that could give you the right answer to an important question in your life. Yours may be a picture of your mother, father, wife, husband—of Benjamin Franklin or Abraham Lincoln. It may be that of a saint.

What will your picture say to you? There is one way to find out. When you are faced with a serious problem or decision, ask your picture a question. Listen for the answer.

Another essential ingredient for changing your world is to have *definiteness of purpose,* one of the 17 principles of success.

Definiteness of purpose is the starting point of all achievement. Definiteness of purpose, *combined with PMA*, is the starting point of all worthwhile achievement. Remember—your world will change whether or not you choose to change it. But you have the power to choose its direction. You can select your own targets. When you determine your definite major aims with PMA, there is a natural tendency for you to use seven of the success principles:

(a) Personal initiative
(b) Self-discipline
(c) Creative vision
(d) Organized thinking
(e) Controlled attention (concentration of effort)
(f) Budgeting of time and money.
(g) Enthusiasm

Robert Christopher had definiteness of purpose with PMA.

Now, let's see how the natural tendencies for these additional principles manifested themselves in this success story. For, like many boys, Bob's imagination was stimulated while he read Jules Verne's thrilling, imaginative story *Around the World in 80 Days*. Bob told us:

"I used to daydream a great deal but when I grew older, I read two books on motivation: *Think and Grow Rich* and *The Magic of Believing*.

"Around the world in 80 days. Now, why couldn't I go around the world on $80.00? I believed that any given aim could be accomplished if I had faith and confidence that it could be. That is: if I started from where I was to get to where I wanted to be.

"I thought: 'Others had worked on freighters to earn their transatlantic passages and hitchhiked all over the world, so why couldn't I?'"

And then Bob took his fountain pen from his pocket and wrote on a piece of note paper a list of the problems with which he would be faced. Also, he made notes of what he thought were workable answers to each.

Now Bob Christopher was an expert photographer and he did have a camera. It was a good one at that. When he reached his decision, he went into action:

(a) Entered a contract with Charles Pfizer Company, a large pharmaceutical company, to collect soil samples from the various countries he intended to visit.

(b) Obtained an international driver's license and a set of maps in return for a promised report on Middle East road conditions.

(c) Picked up seamen's papers.

(d) Obtained a letter from the New York City Police Department to prove that he had no criminal record.

(e) Arranged for a Youth Hostel Membership.

(f) Contacted a freight airline which agreed to transport him by plane over the Atlantic on his promise to obtain photographs which the company intended to use for publicity.

And when his plans were completed, this young man of 26 left New York City by plane with $80.00 in his pocket. *Around the world on $80.00* was his definite major aim. And here are a few of his experiences:

- Had breakfast at Gander, Newfoundland. How did he pay for it? He photographed the cooks in the kitchen. And they were pleased.
- Bought four cartons of American cigarettes at Shannon, Ireland that cost him $4.80. At that time cigarettes were as good as money as a medium of exchange in many countries.
- Arrived at Vienna from Paris. The fee—one carton of cigarettes to the driver.
- Gave the conductor four packs of cigarettes to take him from Vienna to Switzerland on a train through the Alps.
- Rode a bus to Damascus. A policeman in Syria was so proud of the picture that Bob had taken of him that he ordered the bus driver to take him.
- Took a photograph of the president and staff of the Iraq Express Transportation Company. This earned him a ride from Baghdad to Tehran.
- In Bangkok, the owner of a very fine restaurant fed him like a king. For Bob gave him the information he wanted—a detailed description of a specific area and a set of maps.
- Was brought from Japan to San Francisco as a crew member of S.S. *The Flying Spray.*

Around the world in 80 days? No—Robert Christopher went around the world in 84 days. But he did accomplish his objective. He went around the world on $80.00.

THE STARTING POINT OF ALL ACHIEVEMENT

Let us repeat: The starting point of all achievement is definiteness of purpose with PMA. Remember this statement and ask yourself, What is my goal? What do I really want?

Based on the people we see in our PMA Science of Success course, we estimate that 98 out of every 100 persons who are dissatisfied with their world do not have a clear picture in their minds of the world they *would* like for themselves.

Think of it! Think of the people who drift aimlessly through life, dissatisfied, struggling *against* a great many things, but without a clear-cut goal. Can you state, right now, what it is that you want out of life? Fixing your goals may not be easy. It may even involve some painful self-examination. But it will be worth whatever effort it costs, because as soon as you can name your goal, you can expect to enjoy many advantages. These advantages come almost automatically.

1. The first great advantage is that your subconscious mind begins to work under a universal law: "What the mind of man can *conceive* and *believe*—the mind of man can *achieve* with PMA." Because you visualize your intended destination, your subconscious mind is affected by this self-suggestion. It goes to work to help you get there.

2. Because you know what you want, there is a tendency for you to try to get on the right track and head in the right direction. You get into action.

3. Work now becomes fun. You are motivated to pay the price. You budget your time and money. You study, think, and plan. The more you think about your goals, the more enthusiastic you become. And with enthusiasm your desire turns into a *burning* desire.

4. You become alerted to opportunities that will help you achieve your objectives as they present themselves in your

everyday experiences. Because you know what you want, you are more likely to recognize these opportunities.

These four advantages are illustrated by an early experience of the man who was later to become editor of the *Ladies' Home Journal*. Edward Bok came from Holland as a boy with his parents. He was imbued with the idea that someday he was going to run a magazine. With this specific goal before him he was able to seize upon an incident so trivial that with most of us it would have passed unnoticed.

He saw a man open a package of cigarettes, take a slip of paper from it, and drop the paper on the floor. Bok stooped and picked up the scrap of paper. On it was a picture of a famous actress. Below the picture was a statement that this was one of a series. The cigarette buyer was urged to collect the complete set of pictures. Bok turned the piece of paper over and noticed that the back side was perfectly blank.

Bok's mind, filled as it was with a purpose, sensed an opportunity here. He reasoned that the value of the picture enclosed in the package of cigarettes would be greatly enhanced if the blank side were devoted to a brief biography of the person pictured. He went to the lithograph firm which printed the enclosure and explained his idea to the manager. The manager promptly said:

"I'll give you ten dollars each if you will write me a 100-word biography of 100 famous Americans. Send me a list, and group them—you know: presidents, famous soldiers, actors, authors, and so on."

This is the way Edward Bok got his first literary assignment. The demand for his short biographies became so great that he needed help, so he offered his brother five dollars each if he would help him. Before long, Bok had five journalists busy turning out biographies for the lithograph presses. Bok—he was the editor!

You have success born in you. Notice that none of the men we have been talking about had success handed to him on a platter. At first the world was not particularly kind to Edward Bok or Judge Cooper. And yet each carved from the raw material around him a career of great satisfaction. And each one did it by developing the many talents he found within himself.

Everyone has many talents for surmounting his special problems. It is interesting to note that life never leaves us stranded. If life hands us a problem, it hands us also the abilities with which to meet the problem. Our abilities vary, of course, as we are motivated to use them. And even though you are in ill health, you can nonetheless lead a useful and happy life.

A formula to help you change your world. Fortunately not every life is faced with such great difficulties. Yet everyone has problems. And everyone reacts to motivating symbols through suggestion or self-suggestion. A most effective form is a self-motivator deliberately memorized for the purpose of flashing from the subconscious to the conscious in time of need.

I DARE YOU!

What, then, is a formula that can help you change your world? Memorize, understand, and repeat frequently throughout the day: What the mind of man can *conceive* and *believe,* the mind of man can *achieve* with PMA. It is a form of self-suggestion. It is a self-motivator to success. When it becomes a part of you, *you dare to aim higher.*

Bill was a sickly farm boy in the southeastern Missouri country. A dedicated grammar school teacher motivated young William Danforth to change his world. The teacher did this with a challenge: *I Dare You!* "I dare you to become the healthiest boy in school!" *I Dare You!* became William Danforth's self-motivator throughout life.

He became the healthiest boy in his school. Before he died at the age of 85, he helped thousands of other youths to develop good health—and something more: to aspire nobly, to adventure daringly, and to serve humbly. During his long career he never lost a day at work because of illness.

I Dare You! motivated him to build one of America's largest corporations, The Ralston Purina Company. *I Dare You!* motivated him to engage in creative thinking and turn liabilities into assets. *I Dare You!* motivated him to organize The American Youth Foundation: its purpose is to train young men and women in Christian ideals and to prepare them for the responsibilities of life.

I Dare You! motivated William Danforth to write a book entitled *I Dare You!* Today this book is inspiring boys and girls, men and women, to have the courage to make this world a better world to live in.

What a remarkable testimony to the power of a self-motivator to develop a positive mental attitude!

Are you, yourself, ever tempted to blame the world for your failures? If so, pause and reconsider. Does the problem lie with the world, or with you? Dare to learn the 17 success principles! Dare to memorize self-motivators! Dare to apply them with the full assurance that they will work for you just as effectively as they are working every day for hundreds of others.

POINTS TO REMEMBER

1. If you have a problem with something then change it instead of complaining about it.
2. You are the most important person in your life.
3. Identify yourself with a successful image and win over self-doubt.